Tina Louise Kirby Milligan
(615) 852-7710
tina.sittinginmychair@gmail.com
tina.sittinginmychair.com

SITTING IN MY CHAIR

LIFE AFTER TRAUMA WHILE LIVING WITH DISABILITIES

**The Autobiography of
TINA LOUISE KIRBY MILLIGAN**

© 2017 Tina Louise Milligan

All Rights Reserved

ISBN-13: 978-0-578-45995-0

© 2017 *Sitting in My Chair*
Text, Photographs & Artwork
United States of America
Registration Number: TXu 2-134-732
February 7, 2019

All rights reserved. No portion of this book may be reproduced, stored in a retrieval system, or transmitted in any form or by any means. Not by electronic, mechanical, photocopied, recording, scanning, or other, without prior written permission from the Author.

Published by: Tina Milligan, © 2019

Dear Reader,

 I have worked on this book for over a year. You will occasionally see flashback and flash-forward content as I tell my story. This book is not a work of fiction. It is a true story about my life. I am not writing the story of anyone else that came across my path over the last 41 years. Their journey is their story to tell, not mine.

 I want to share my journey with others, not to seek revenge, but rather to bring awareness and support to fellow warriors. I had to use pseudonyms to protect innocent bystanders and to stop those who would attempt to gain from the pain they inflicted. Names have either been omitted or changed. I have given myself the name Elizabeth Clarke.

 I am opening myself up in a way that can never be undone. While I hold the guilty responsible, I have forgiven their transgressions so that I can heal my wounds. Never again will they be able to hurt me.

 I pray that my journey will help others who are walking the same road find light in the darkness.

Tina Louise Milligan

NOTE TO MYSELF

October 2017

I have visions of myself kicking and screaming. Then, the voices of war between good and evil start inside my head.

"Elizabeth, you need to write this book! The family business is struggling. Daddy is on the road all the time, and your stepmom's health continues to decline. You're the glue, and you're so thin that you can barely keep paper together anymore. On top of that, you're fighting a new battle called Multiple Sclerosis."

When I write, I feel as though I am standing naked while my blood pours onto the pages. The thought of strangers knowing everything fills me with raging anxiety. This is going to be the hardest thing I have ever had to do. Here they come again. The loud voices inside my head.

"Just stop, Elizabeth. Stop right now. Don't write this.... the truth could ....it could hurt the people you love. Elizabeth, there you go again.... STOP BEING NEGATIVE!!! Remember Elizabeth? Remember college? Ms. Lewald said you were a marvelous writer."

Ok, here goes nothing! See you on the other side....

I dedicate this book to my husband Edgar, as he always encouraged me to tell my story.
I love you Edgar.

~Prologue~

    I take my chair with me on days when my legs are refusing to corporate. On one particular day, during my trip to New York City in October 2017, I was sitting in my chair, reflecting on my ancestors. It was overwhelming. I was on Ellis Island. I was sitting in the very spot that my great-great-grandparents walked as they arrived in America for the first time in 1905.

    Thinking about the courage that it took for them to come to a new place where they knew no one, changed my perspective on my entire life. I realized that my ancestors were brave men and women. It was at that moment that I decided it was time to use that strength to write my story. Grab your favorite chair, and get comfortable while you join me on my journey.

Contents

It's a girl - 1977 – My Birth

Chapter 1 - 1978 - First year of my Life "Normal."

Chapter 2 - 1979 - Second Year of my Life "Living in Florida."

Chapter 3 - 1980 - Third Year of my Life "Abuse Started."

Chapter 4 - 1981 - Fourth Year of my Life "Toys & Candy."

Chapter 5 - 1982 - Fifth Year of my Life "Faded Memories."

Chapter 6 - 1983 - Sixth Year of my Life "Kindergarten."

Chapter 7 - 1984 - Seventh Year of my Life "Good Memories."

Chapter 8 - 1985 - Eighth Year of my Life "Baby Sister & Drunk Drivers."

Chapter 9 - 1986 - Ninth Year of my Life "Demons walk at night."

Chapter 10 - 1987 - Tenth Year of my Life "Busch Gardens."

Chapter 11 - 1988 - Eleventh Year of my Life "Burned my Hand."

Chapter 12 - 1989 - Twelfth Year of my Life "My Father's Betrayal."

Chapter 13 - 1990 - Thirteenth Year of my Life "Middle School."

Chapter 14 - 1991 - Fourteenth Year of my Life "The Mental Hospital."

Chapter 15 - 1992 - Fifteenth Year of my Life "Summer to Remember."

Chapter 16 - 1993 - Sixteenth Year of my Life "Marriage & Divorce."

Chapter 17 - 1994 - Seventeenth Year of my Life "Longing for Him."

Chapter 18 - 1995 - Eighteenth Year of my Life "I am a Mom."

Chapter 19 - 1996 - Nineteenth Year of my Life "My Son is born."

Chapter 20 - 1997 - Twentieth Year of my Life "Maple Avenue."

Chapter 21 - 1998 - Twenty-First Year of my Life "My Baby girl is born."

Chapter 22 - 1999 - Twenty-Second Year of my Life "Moving."

Chapter 23 - 2000 - Twenty-Third Year of my Life "College."

Chapter 24 - 2001 - Twenty-Fourth Year of my Life "Lies & Cancer."

Chapter 25 - 2002 - Twenty-Fifth Year of my Life "Hysterectomy."

Chapter 26 - 2003 - Twenty-Sixth Year of my Life "Rainbow City."

Chapter 27 - 2004 - Twenty-Seventh Year of my Life "Disney World."

Chapter 28 - 2005 - Twenty- Eighth Year of my Life "Mountains."

Chapter 29 - 2006 - Twenty-Ninth Year of my Life "Pain & Park Rd."

Chapter 30 - 2007 - Thirtieth Year of my Life "My Nightmare."

Chapter 31 - 2008 - Thirty-First Year of my Life "Panther Creek."

Chapter 32 - 2009 - Thirty-Second Year of my Life "The Devil is real."

Chapter 33 - 2010 - Thirty-Third Year of my Life "New Beginnings."

Chapter 34 - 2011 - Thirty-Fourth Year of my Life "Back to College."

Chapter 35 - 2012 - Thirty-Fifth Year of my Life "History Repeats."

Chapter 36 - 2013 - Thirty-Sixth Year of my Life "Justice for my Child."

Chapter 37 - 2014 - Thirty-Seventh Year of my Life "Sulfur Ridge."

Chapter 38 - 2015 - Thirty-Eighth Year of my Life "I'm a Grandma."

Chapter 39 - 2016 - Thirty-Ninth Year of my Life "Depression."

Chapter 40 - 2017 - Fortieth Year of my Life "New York, New York."

Chapter 41 - 2018 - Forty-First Year of my Life "Truth is Pain."

The End – 2019

MY BIRTH

It's a Girl!

1977 and President Carter is in the White House. Elvis made his last entrance, and my mom was overdue!

I was born on a snowy December morning, in a small hospital located in McMinnville, Tennessee. The nurse said I came out smiling. (Note to self, I was once a happy child). My parents took me home to our tiny trailer nestled in the backcountry of Walling, Tennessee. My mom says that I was a healthy baby girl with big blue eyes and curly hair.

I was also a rainbow child, as my mother had gone through a miscarriage before having me. I often wished my mom had given birth to the boy that she had miscarried. Through the years, I felt that he would have protected me.

My mom said my birth filled her with great joy. She would always add that my father never wanted children as he saw children as a financial burden. To this day, financial troubles cause him anxiety and stress. Tension runs in my family's bloodline!

Although I was born a healthy child, my father was distraught that I wasn't a boy. If you know anything about country folk, then you know having a son to pass on the family name is a big deal! When I think I am not good enough, I often think "if only I had been a boy." However, men have their own set of problems, so I doubt that it would have changed things much.

My mother was excited to finally be a mother. She actually named me after the famous movie star from the television show Gilligan's Island. I really believe that this part of my life was relatively normal. My aunt and uncles would often tell my mother that I had beautiful features.

Flash-forward: Mom says that she loves my sister and me, but if she had known what she knows now that she would have waited to have children.

My dad's mother, "Grandma Abigail," lived in Tampa, Florida, with my Step-Grandfather, and she would often call to check on me. She told me many disturbing stories about my childhood. It didn't take much to bring her to tears when we would talk about the past.

I do not have any pictures of my grandparents holding me as a baby. I used to assume that they didn't rush to the hospital to welcome me into the world. However, my mothers' parents were there the entire time. I never heard the story of my birth from Grandma Abigail, and my mother said she was not at the hospital. I know it was winter and it was snowing...so maybe travel was an issue? I am a grandma now, so I just can't imagine not being there the moment my grandchild comes into the world.

Flash-Forward: I got to experience this in 2018, and it was awful. Dakota did not want me in the room for the birth of my first granddaughter. I sat in the car and cried for hours. A few days later, on Thanksgiving Day, I got to meet my granddaughter, and it was a beautiful experience. However, I hope none of you ever have to sit alone and cry while your grandchild is being born.

Mom tells me that she was in labor for 14 hours, then the doctor had to do an emergency cesarean. That tells me that my dad's parents had plenty of time to show up and be there for my mom. I mean, my mom was having surgery. Why weren't they at the hospital?

I do not want to bore you with my assumptions. After all, only my dad's parents know why they didn't show up. This is an example of my first bad habit. I overthink everything and often make excuses for people.

So, right here…right now I am just going to scream it out! MY DAD'S PARENTS SHOULD HAVE BEEN THERE WHEN I WAS BORN!

Over the years, when I had severe bouts of depression, I thought how I wished I had been the rainbow child. I know my brother would have had a much better childhood. All I ever wanted was my father's love. During my search for photos, I could not find any baby pictures with my dad and me.

Many jokes have been made over the years that I always wonder if he is my biological father. He dated many women, so I have to wonder why he never got anyone else pregnant. My mom says I am crazy, but crazier things have happened in my life. President Carter is in the White House. Elvis made his last entrance, and my mom was overdue!

"THE FARM" - Walling, Tennessee

CHAPTER ONE
First Year of my Life
"Normal"

1978 and the very first Garfield comic was published. This is also the year that we got the first woman astronaut in the USA, and some of my favorite movies like Grease were on the big screen. I was growing by leaps and bounds, and everyone loved my curls.

I do not remember the first year of my life, but my grandma Abigail would occasionally tell me stories of a time when she came to visit me.

She said that I would be sitting in the middle of the kitchen table with cereal. She would always add that I was in a urine-soaked diaper, and she had to wake my mother from a deep sleep to take care of me.

Flash-Forward: My mother said the above incident did not happen. My grandma is not here to argue the fact, and forty-one years have come and gone since grandma Abigail said this happened.

I do have memories of myself getting out of bed in the early morning hours looking for food. My parents were poor, and we didn't have much when I was small.

Flash-forward: I know my personality now, so I am guessing I did eat in the early morning hours. I am working on this, so don't judge...HAHAHA

As I look at the pictures from this year, I keep looking at my little hands and how I had them drawn up into a bit of a fist. Is that the fighter in me? Maybe it was early signs of Multiple Sclerosis? Either way, those hands helped me through life, and I thank God that I have them.

I also remember my mom's parents. They lived in Monterey, Tennessee, but have since passed on. I miss them so much. They were always so loving towards me. I remember how their house smelled of old tobacco and coffee. To this day, I love coffee and the occasional smoke. I quit smoking cigarettes many years ago, but now we have these things called Vapors and CBD oil. They are fantastic for anxiety and pain.

My mom's parents worked hard to take care of my uncle, who was paralyzed from a work accident. He lived with them, and I always remember how he smelled of marijuana. I think it was probably much better for him than the pain medications. Those pills eat up a person's stomach, and they are what killed my mom's father.

Flash-forward: We currently have an opioid crisis in America. I have to take them for my pain, and I am terrified of addiction. I have never had a problem with addiction, but the documentary "Painkiller: Inside the Opioid Crisis" caused my anxiety to escalate.

The next picture was taken at my mom's parents' house in Monterey in 1978. I was lying on a blanket basking in the sun. I look like such a happy baby. I like to think that everything was peaceful in my life at this point.

Tina Louise Kirby - 1978

CHAPTER TWO
Second Year of my Life
"Living in Florida"

1979 and "Little House on the Prairie" played on television, with the Walton's, and everyone loved Happy Days.

Flash-forward: My mom said we moved to Florida when I was a year and a half old. My dad told her the jobs were better there, and I was told that he wanted to be closer to his mom.

The only real memory I have from this time in my life scares me to this day. In Florida, they have palmetto bugs. My father used to think it was funny to scare me with them. It might be why I have a massive phobia of insects and spiders.

During our time living in Florida, my dad told me that I almost drowned in the ocean because my mom wasn't watching me. She pulled me out of the water, but the blame game always makes my parents' stories sound different. They would blame each other for every mistake because it couldn't be that life was hard sometimes. No... That wasn't possible. It had to be someone's fault!

We only stayed in Florida for 3 months, then it was back to the farm in Walling. My mother hated being away from her family, and she felt so alone in Florida. She said it was some of the loneliest times of her life.

Flash-Forward - My mother told me that I wrote with crayons on the wall, and my dad gave me a good beating. It left a mark on my eye, and my grandma Abigail chewed him out for his behavior. When she told me this, I couldn't help but think back and wish we had stayed in Florida. I know I hate sand, but it would have been better than years of abuse.

I have a few flashbacks of being small, like when dad bought me my first bowling set for Christmas. I remember tossing the ball down the hall in our little trailer. That is probably the only Christmas I ever had with my family. It wasn't long after this that I recall a Brother from our local Kingdom Hall teaching me a bible scripture.

"Psalms 83:18 - May people know that you, whose name is Jehovah, you alone are the Highest over all the earth."

I do wish my dad had learned a few verses like the one about anger and the one about adultery. Our family could have really used those. I know you can sense my sarcasm here, but many times I find that we are always learning things that will never be of any good use to us in life. When you set out to help someone, always remember to actually focus on the real problems. Knowledge is useless if it isn't applied.

At some point during this year, my father burned my toys. He ripped the head of my doll off in the kitchen. I have horrible flashbacks of my baby doll and the anger in my father's face. I think my grandma mailed me these gifts from Florida. You know my grandma always thought my mother gave those gifts away to her family. She never knew the truth, and my heart could not bear to tell her before she died. She had already lost the love of her life and her youngest son, so I just could not break her heart anymore.

I have to pause right now. This is so hard to write. I love my parents, and to this day, I don't understand why my father had such anger in his heart. I have a few theories, like how he was trying to quit smoking, and I heard rumors that he was abused as a child. All I know is that I don't understand. Maybe one day, he will tell me.

Flash-forward: (September 5th, 2018 - Yesterday, my sister came over, and we had the best night going through pictures, eating cake, and getting very intoxicated. My youngest daughter is quite the bartender. However, the next morning, while I was taking a bath, my poor baby sister was sick. I know she loves drinking, but it doesn't love her so much. While alcohol can help some, it is poison to people who have a chronic illness like Hidradenitis Suppurativa or Multiple Sclerosis. I have both of these autoimmune diseases, and inflammation makes the pain much worse after a night of drinking.)

Tina Louise Kirby - 1979 age 2

TAKE A DEEP BREATH

CHAPTER THREE
Third Year of my Life
"Sexual Abuse Started"

1980 and Ronald Reagan was elected, and the talking Alf was in toy stores. I lived the first years of my life on the family farm. My memories tend to come and go, but I have a few haunting memories that rarely leave my thoughts.

Flashback: I am standing behind my great grandma's house, and I can see the grapevines. Then I am in the barn. I smell the hogs and the corn. Suddenly Richard is standing in front of me with candy, and he is pulling at my panties.

This brings me so much sadness because I loved Ma & Pa. Knowing that I was molested on their farm makes me question my parents even more. Where were they? Why were my parents not around to stop this from happening? Maybe they were at work or inside the house?

Flash-Forward: My mother said Ma and Pa (My dad's paternal grandparents) were babysitting me on their farm while my parents worked. This was also when the sexual abuse started.

A few years ago, my great Aunt and uncle sold Ma & Pa's farm, and I was outraged. I felt like if anyone deserved to profit from the sale of that land, it wasn't my Aunt. I felt myself and the other girls who were victimized there during the '80s deserved compensation. However, I kept that to myself because I do not want the confrontation with my elders. That generation in my family never protected me, and I doubt they will start now.

As I look at pictures from this year, I wonder how I could even smile. I am guessing the photographer knew what they were doing to get such a smile from me. I have accepted that at such a young age, I didn't realize that what my step-uncles did to me was wrong, so I didn't feel abused.

Is it possible that if you do not understand that something is wrong that it doesn't harm you mentally the way it does if you know it is wrong? I don't know, but you will see that it touched every part of my life as an adolescent.

I have no memories of bedtime stories, birthdays, or happy events during 1980, but I did find pictures. Occasionally, I remember a hole in my bedroom floor and how my kitten would come up through the floor, which brought me great comfort when I was scared.

I turned three years old in December and believe the next pictures were the last taken before the abuse started.

Tina Louise Kirby Age 2 ½ - 1980

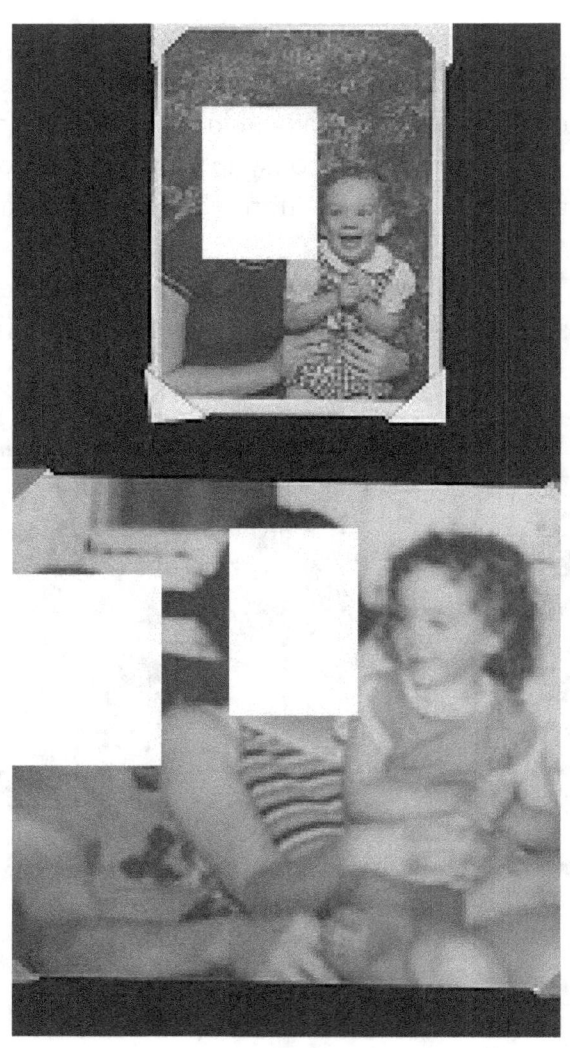

CHAPTER FOUR
Fourth Year of my Life
"Toys & Candy"

1981 and Sandra Day O'Connor was appointed the first female justice to the United States Supreme Court, and Dolly Parton was working 9 to 5.

Flashback: I remember my mom yell my name. Elizabeth .... Elizabeth ...I run into the house as my mother calls for me. I pranced in the house like a little princess. My mother asked me why my step uncles were giving me toys and candy all the time. Elizabeth ANSWER ME, she yelled!

I looked down and tugged at my pants. My mom screams, "Thomas come here.... come here! Come here, NOW"! After hearing my mom's cries, my father ran into the house. He had a look of panic on his face. Her words seemed so scary, and I didn't understand why she was crying.

My dad's face filled with rage, and then he rushed out of the trailer and jumped in his car. I still remember the sound of the gravel as my dad left the driveway.

I was told that my dad stormed into my grandfather's house. I imagine he said something like, "Do you have any idea what the boys have been doing to my daughter?" but I am not sure. I was told that my Grandpa listened to my dad, and then he took a stick from the counter and started beating Richard, then he dragged him outside and into the vehicle. They drove over to our home, and this is when my Flashback begins again.

Flashback: I am looking out the door of our home. I can see Richard walk to the door, and he apologizes. I wondered why he was sorry. I only say sorry when I do something bad. Maybe he isn't supposed to give me toys?

Flash-forward: November 24, 2017 - Breath. Corn and manure. Shadows between the slats. I am in the barn. It is cold, and I am scared.

My mother told me that dad would lock me in the barn when I was terrible. I have no idea what I did wrong. It is repulsive that my father thought it was ok to lock me in a barn to punish me. To make things worse, the men running around the outside of the barn, making noises to scare me, were the very men who were giving me candy to trick me into showing them my private parts.

Flashback - I am being forced to drink warm urine. Well, that is what I think it is. I had problems wetting the bed so my parents would make warm salt water and make me believe it was urine.

When I think back on this story, I wonder if my parents were possibly on drugs. I love them, but seriously this is insanity!!

It wasn't long before my dad moved us to town. His father did not like that my dad was studying with the Jehovah's Witnesses. Grandpa fired my dad, and so they left the farm. I remember our small apartment and my mom's record collection. She had music from so many artists. Credence was my favorite, and sitting on the dock of the bay sent me to dreamland many nights.

I have spent many hours going through photo albums that belonged to my grandma and my parents. I cannot seem to find any from this year. I will turn four in December, so that means from age three to age four, no photos can be located. I continue to wonder why, but I assume that it was because I was not a happy child.

Flash-forward: Today is September 9, 2018, and my mom came to lunch with her new boyfriend. Edgar made ribs and pumpkin pie. It was delicious! Afterward, we sat in the living room talking about one thing, then another. The conversation of my book came up, and she said once, when I was 3 years old, I pulled the television over on my face. She took me to the hospital, and they had to give me shots to calm me down. After they stitched up my lip, we headed home. I then proceeded to pull all of my stitches from my mouth. Mom refused to take me back and said I would just have to settle with a swollen lip. I remember the story, but not the actual event.

I believe the next picture was taken after I sliced my lip open as it looks like my mouth is injured in this picture.

CHAPTER FIVE
Fifth Year of my Life
"Faded Memories"

1982 and Ronald Reagan is now in the White House, and Cheese puffs only cost $0.89. I was unable to find many memories or pictures from this year, but I will continue to work on it. I know that because I was born in December that I had to start school a year later than children my age. I would be almost six before I started Kindergarten.

Flashback: This is the year that I got Tigger. My very first grey cat. Yes, I was five years old! That is a beautiful memory. Also, we were living in town, so the abuse was limited. I have memories of walking the sidewalks and getting large cookies from Hardees. Maybe this year was one of the few happy years of my childhood. Moving to town was probably the best decision my father ever made for me.

The next picture is a mystery, it might have been Christmas, 1982. I would have just turned 5 years old. However, that is confusing because my dad was studying with the Jehovah's Witnesses, and they didn't celebrate holidays.

My mother did tell me that for years, she celebrated in secret with her parents. She has always felt that your walk with God is your own, and no man should be making spiritual decisions for you. I believe that God sends people into your life to help you on your journey. However, I do not think that we need to adopt their beliefs unless we want to. I am all about free will.

I have many friends and family who practice the Jehovah's Witness faith, and they are some of the most loving and beautiful people I know. I cherish the time they have spent with me over the years.

I have decided not to practice any religion. I have my own personal relationship with God. I occasionally share my beliefs, but I never push them on anyone. True Jehovah's Witnesses are not mean, nor do they attempt to force their beliefs on you.

Flash-Forward: It is now 2019, and #metoo is everywhere. I have watched many documentaries on sex abuse in families and religious organizations. I do not tell you this to make you paranoid. I am telling you this because evil has a way of breaching the most sacred of walls. This includes the family home, close relatives, friends, religious organizations, schools/school buses, doctors' offices, military, the workplace, Universities, the entertainment industry, and sporting teams. We trust too much in our society, and the screens keep us preoccupied. Satan doesn't want us to pay attention to his wicked deeds.

I do not recognize this house or the tree, but I believe my grandma sent me the Mickey shirt from Florida. My dad's mom was always good about sending me gifts.

Winter is my favorite time of year.

CHAPTER SIX
"Kindergarten"
Sixth Year of my Life

1983 and the world population is at 4.68

billion, and a 5.2 magnitude earthquake hits Central Park. This year I started Elementary School. I remember I poked paper balls into my ears with a pencil.

This is also the year I got into trouble with Stephen behind the school. We were playing the "you show me yours, and I will show you mine game." I think we were both just curious as we neither one had siblings.

Flash-forward: I recently found Stephen on Facebook, and we have been talking. He is still a beautiful person. I wish we had grown up together. I hate that he had to move away. I used to daydream about a life where I wasn't abused and how Stephen would have taken me to the prom.

The rest of this year is totally blank, and I would be lying if I said I remembered anything else. My mother said I was always getting into trouble, but never did my parents suspect that I was still being molested. I can picture the classrooms and the gym in my mind, but now my old school is the YMCA.

Flash-forward: November 30, 2018- I am waiting for my sister in my van at Walgreens, and I thought now would be a good time to write. I look over, and there is Mrs. Jones loading Mr. Jones into her van. I seriously jumped out and talked to her. It was so awesome to have a good conversation with the lady who lived next door to us all my years on the farm. I told her I would come down for a cup of coffee one day, and she seemed pleased with that suggestion. However, the more I think about it, the probability of me going is slim to none. Anytime I get near the farm, I have weeks of depression.

Tina Louise Kirby – 1983 - Kindergarten

Do You Remember your first crush?

CHAPTER SEVEN
"1ˢᵗ Grade"
7th Year of my Life
"Good Memories"

1984 and Paul & Linda McCartney were arrested for possession of cannabis, and Apple unveiled the Macintosh personal computer. Kindergarten is over, and I will be starting 1st grade. Recently while going through my grandma's photos, I found pictures from the summer of 1984.

We were visiting my grandma, and I looked so happy. This was probably the best summer I had up to this point in my life. I was away from the abuse and around love. Grandpa Leo was always so funny, kind, and giving. He also had a way of bringing out the good in my parents. I do not remember my dad ever hit me while we were around my grandparents.

My mother never really smiled much, but this year she was glowing like an angel. In the pictures below, my parents look so happy. It only confuses me even more. I know that the environment changes people. Many people have said that people are "born this way" or that it is in their genes, but I am convinced that a positive environment can recreate a happy person.

Flash-Forward: If you find yourself around negative people all of the time, don't be surprised if you end up depressed. Negativity breeds depression. I know the doctors say it is a chemical imbalance in the brain, but my experience has shown that it is all about the company you keep!

My childhood best friend sent me the annual pictures she found of us in first and second grade. I sure miss her right now. Jersey seems so far away.

I am unsure about this picture, and there are no dates on it. I am wearing winter clothing, and I had just lost a tooth. I want to say this is the late fall of 1984 because I still had all my teeth in my school picture from this year. In 1985, I had two large front teeth. This photo will probably always be a mystery.

Flashback: Where the gravestones are used to be our first apartment, and those stairs are where I ran the day Booger first tried to get his hands on me. I don't remember much about this day, but I do remember running away from him.

Be careful when you're walking alone…

CHAPTER EIGHT
"2nd Grade"
Eighth Year of my Life
"Baby Sister & Drunk Drivers"

1985 and the "Color Purple" premieres and Nintendo releases the NES. My mom would come down with rheumatic fever and almost died. She was a fighter, though. This year would prove to be one of the hardest on my mom. I remember begging God to make her better while crying myself to sleep.

I was excited that I would soon be a big sister. However, during the last month of my mom's pregnancy, we were hit by a drunk driver. I have powerful memories of this accident.

Flashback: We were coming down Bon Air Mountain. We had just left a baby shower, and I saw a car swerving. I said mom, "We better put our seat belts on," and the moment I heard my seatbelt click, we were hit with such force, and the station wagon went spinning. I do not remember his name, but I remember being so angry. We were standing in the emergency room, and I looked over and saw him. He was on the edge of the hospital gurney repeating "what happened" over and over. I yelled, "you idiot, you almost killed us! That's what happened". My mom was shaken up, but she survived with no real injury.

Kathy was born on September 12, 1985. I loved her so much. Dad bought her a real tall Victorian dresser, and we carried it in the house before mom came home. I decided to cut my own hair, and I have no idea why. My parents made me take school pictures anyway. I put on the big smile of courage.

I finally felt like I had a friend when mom brought Kathy home. We lived on Clark Street in Sparta, Tennessee. It was an adorable little house sitting on the corner. I loved living in town because I could get the big cookies at Hardee's all the time. I had a big backyard, and I felt safe until I met the neighbor man. My parents were still studying with the Jehovah's Witnesses, so my dad was super strict, but I was allowed to walk in our neighborhood alone. Even that wasn't safe because a pervert noticed.

Flashback: I remember a neighbor man trying to molest me. This year was very confusing for me because I got into trouble for so many things. I was told that I decided to touch one of my female friends sexually, so I couldn't have friends over anymore. I also have a memory of a big red dog. I loved him so much, but he belonged to someone else, and they took him back.

    I think back to my friend coming over, and I wonder why no one suspected that I was being molested. All the signs were there from bed wetting to cutting my hair. I radiated signs of an abused child. People have tried to call it incest over the years because it was my step-uncles, but I refer to them as monsters when I speak about what happened to me.

Clark Street, Sparta, Tennessee

West Sparta Elementary, Sparta, Tennessee

CHAPTER NINE
"3rd Grade"
Ninth Year of my Life
"Demons walk at night"

1986 and nuclear power station in

Chernobyl, Ukraine, exploded, and the stage musical "Phantom of the Opera" debuts in London. I still lived in the house on Clark Street in Sparta, Tennessee. I was quite the actress.

This would be the year that I fell and hit my knee on the fireplace. Mom jerked my knee thinking it was out of place, but it only hurt worse. We went to dinner at Bonanza in Cookeville. In the middle of dinner, I noticed my knee was swollen. It got so tight that my dad had to cut off my pants. After they dropped Kathy off in Monterey with my grandparents, we went back to the hospital.

Flashback: I went to the fair with my grandpa and then we went back to the farm. I was sleeping on the couch, and someone woke me up. Next, I am on the floor on my hands and knees. Someone is hurting my bottom. It smells like Richard, but it could have been William.

Flash-forward: October 8, 2018 - I have been dreading this day. We are back to the night that someone sodomized me while I was sleeping. It is a horrible memory, and I feel sick when the flashbacks come out of nowhere. There were only three men in the house, my grandpa, Richard, and William. My grandfather never touched me inappropriately, so it had to be one of the step uncles.

I have to take a break. I feel sick.

Flashback: There once sat an empty lot where someone parked single house trailers. I was always a curious child, so one day, I went looking, and Booger must have seen me because he followed me inside one of the trailers. I remember there is a mattress on the floor, and I wondered who could be sleeping here. I ran out of the trailer.

Empty Lot on the corner of Emma L Officer Street and West Bockman Way, Sparta, Tennessee

This was my second and final run-in with this boy. He was a young black male that they called "Booger." To this day, I have no idea why, nor do I want to find out. The last time I heard, he was listed as a sex offender and living in the White County Jail.

There have been other rumors that he was a big drug dealer in the area, but he knows never to come around me. We have a clear understanding that I shoot and ask questions later when it comes to men who assaulted me over the years.

I got an email a few years ago, and a dear childhood friend told me a story. I am in the basement of her house, and I jump on top of her and say, "let's make love." It was totally random, and it shocked her at the time. She said I was around ten years old. I still have to wonder how no one had a clue that someone had seriously messed up my little mind. But, if anyone noticed, they failed to do anything about it, so the abuse continued.

I have wanted to write this book for over twenty years, but fear kept my mouth shut. Don't ever let anyone hold you silent. I know it is scary, but you deserve to speak your truth.

Flashback: Mom put Kathy and me in the bath. She was going to talk to dad about getting our layaway out at Walmart. I remember getting out of the tub and going into the living room to get mom when I saw my mom with her mouth on my dad's private parts. I got a good beating for getting out of the tub and walking in on my parents.

CHAPTER TEN
"4th Grade"
Tenth Year of my Life
"Busch Gardens"

1987 and this year was filled with adventure as we went to Busch Gardens in Florida, and I got to ride a roller coaster with my dad. I look so happy in pictures. There isn't even a hint that I had been sexually abused in the photos. I started a new school called Woodland Park.

Flashback: Dad beat me for putting up a small Christmas tree in my room. I went to school and did a cartwheel, and the teacher saw the bruises. Children's Services investigated and took pictures but did not remove me from our home.

    I remember that year more than any year because it was when I realized that the police do not always protect children. I also realized that religion gave cover to parents who beat their children.

    I am not talking cynically about the Jehovah's Witnesses here, but I am stating a fact about religions. I know people have turned a blind eye, and children fell through the cracks at an alarming rate. I mean, think about it. I had tons of people around me, and my great Aunt worked for Children's Services in Michigan. My grandmother was like the FBI, but still, they did nothing.

I mentally dealt with this by telling myself that God has a plan for me, and these things had to happen for that plan to be fulfilled. Now I know that Satan was out for blood because my heart was pure when it came to my love for Christ Jesus and Jehovah God.

Mental Illness is not as cut and dry as many think it is either. It can be found in the most unexpected places within a family. A parent tends to practice the same parenting as their parents, and often it continues the cycle of abuse.

Please seek counseling if you have been abused. Do not ever let the cycle of abuse continue. It will only add to your internal pain and steal moments that you can never get back. Before you even think about loving someone else or becoming a parent, please fix yourself. Don't let the monsters ruin another life!

Roller Coaster with dad at Busch Gardens – 1987

Like a roll coaster, in life there are times of highs and lows, times of peace and fear, and times of good and evil! Tina Milligan – 2019

CHAPTER ELEVEN
"5ᵗʰ Grade"
Eleventh Year of my Life
"Burned my Hand"

1988 and Andre beats Hulk Hogan, and three of my favorite people, Hank Williams Jr, Randy Travis, and Reba McEntire, win at the country music awards. My life is fixing to change for the worse.

Dad made a deal with the man who bought our family farm from my grandfather. We move from the Clark Street house and head back out into the country. My parents bought a new double-wide trailer, and we start working at the festivals and flea markets.

Flash-forward: I use the word flower when I am talking about my genitalia. Society tends to use shock words or vulgar words to talk about our bodies. I now have a great love and respect for my body, so I talk about it in a more nurturing way. I really think all women should because we set an example for the entire world. We do birth the men, and we raise the men to become future husbands and fathers. Our influence and tolerance shape future generations in so many ways.

The next flashback is one of the most horrifying from my memory. I wonder what happened and where were my undergarments, but the mind is frozen in time. To be honest, I don't want to remember what happened because I am sure it was terrifying.

Flashback: I am sitting in red dirt outside of my grandparent's home. I look down, and I see my grandpa's dog lick my swollen flower.

I used to cry when I thought about the above flashback, but now I think the dog was trying to care for me because I was injured. I no longer feel nasty or dirty about this memory because I see how loving and nurturing animals can be when you're hurt.

So many things went wrong in my life this year. I was bitten by my grandpa's dog after I had been holding my rabbits. My step-grandmother Helen did not take me to the hospital, and my mom was furious. My mom came home and got me medical attention.

I was left alone way too much. Helen was supposed to be watching me, but she always seemed to be cooking or missing in action. I feel like she knew something was wrong, but since she has now passed on, I cannot ask her for the truth.

I have the give the photographer five stars here because he captured a perfect illusion.

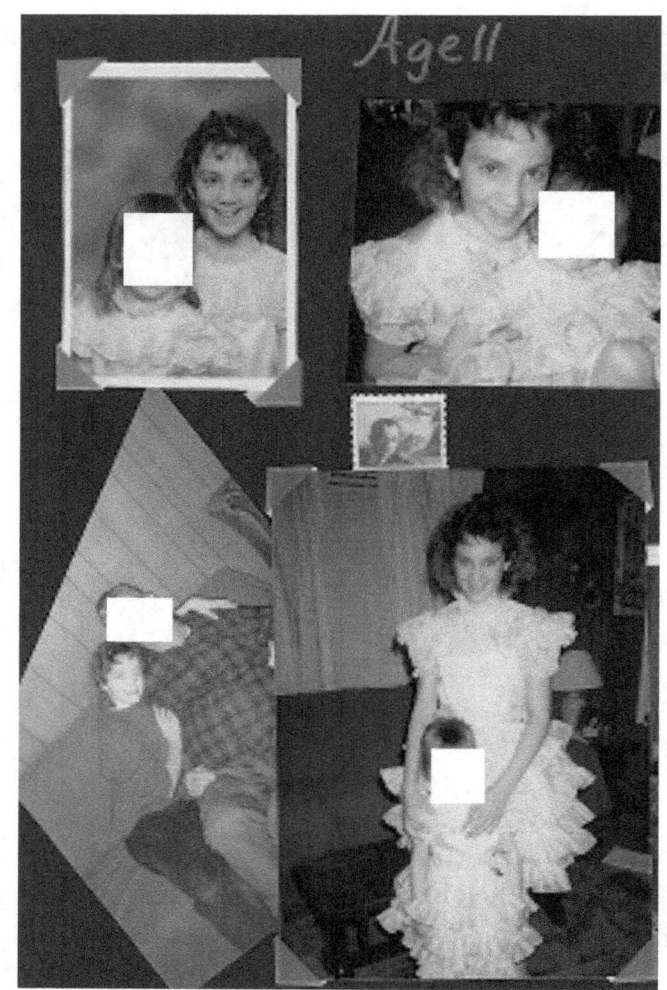

My Moms Dad & Me. I sure miss you, grandpa.

The bottom picture below is a picture of the time that I told my dad that I didn't leave the stove on. Yes, that is right. I slapped my hand on the stove to prove him wrong, and he snapped a picture.

Not everything is funny. Sometimes your ignorance is painful, and you need love, not humor. – Tina Milligan 2019

CHAPTER TWELVE
"6th Grade"
Twelfth Year of my Life
"My father's Betrayal"

1989 and George H. W. Bush was

elected President. My Step uncles continued to touch me any chance they got. I almost felt invisible unless someone was hitting me or using me as a means of pleasure. If I was alone, then I was a target.

My parents were fighting all the time. I would try to hide away in my bedroom with all my pictures of New Kids on the Block & Paula. It was my only escape.

Flashback: My father is giving a guitar lesson in our RV at the Baxter flea market. I walk in on him getting oral sex from a woman. She wasn't my mother. I slammed the door and felt sick.

Flash-forward: This would be the second time that I saw my father getting oral sex in my life. I guess that is why I hate it so much, and for the last 10 years, I have not even engaged in the behavior. My husband is very loving when it comes to this issue, so I do not have to explain myself all the time.

This year I ate more sugar and watched more MTV & Horror movies and played more violent video games at the "good kids" house than I did at the "bad kids" house. My after-school center played more MTV videos than I ever saw anywhere else, but still, at home, life was super strict. I was a child with bedtime, and tons of rules, but my body was the punching bag for my dad and pleasure center for my step-uncles.

Flash-forward: I wanted my writing to be accurate, so I looked up the obituary for the one step-uncle who died a few years ago. I always assumed my step-uncles were twin brothers but nope. William is the younger brother. They were born in 1967 & 1969. They were around the ages of thirteen and eleven when they started molesting me, but they were adult men when they committed sodomy and rape. So, they should be in jail right now. Knowing what I know now, I feel that this is where my family, The Department of Children's Services, Betsy Dunn, and Bill Gibson, dropped the ball big time.

If I remember correctly, these photos were taken at Central View Elementary.

This picture shows the sadness that I was feeling.
It is one of the only ones that captured my inner emotion.

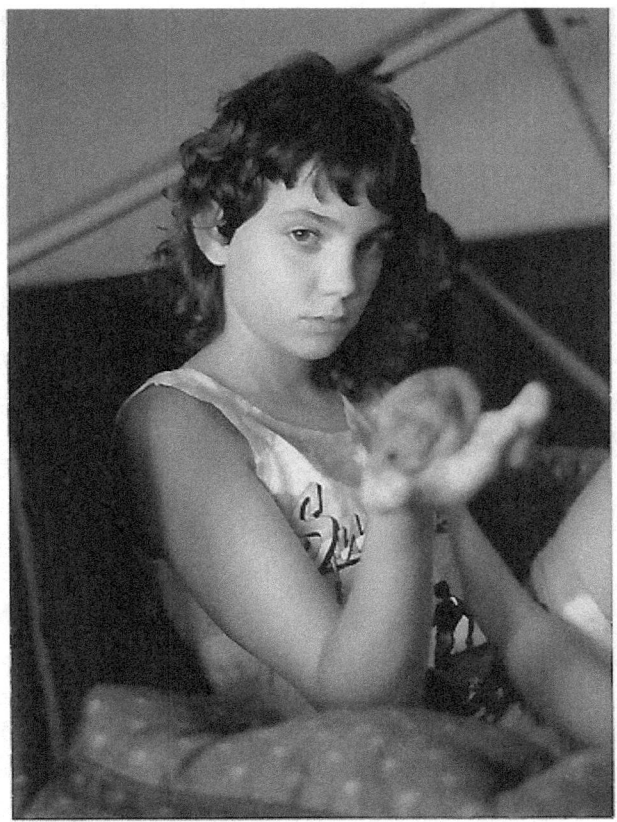

Pictures are the perfect illusion when it comes to child abuse. In one photo, a family looks perfect, but it's the moments at home that capture the raw details. Tina Milligan – 2019

CHAPTER THIRTEEN
"7th Grade"
Thirteenth Year of my Life
"Middle School"

1990 and George Bush is in the White House. I was so excited to start Middle School. I had made some friends, and my long hair made me popular with the hair spray girls. Boys were continually sending me notes, but I only liked one boy named Jeremy. He had blonde hair and blue eyes, and I got to see him in band class. I was playing the snare drum.

There was also a guy named Adam, a tall, dark-haired wild boy who had his eyes on me. He would flirt with me, but I thought he was dangerous.

Flashback: During afternoon band practice, Jeremy decided to break up with me. I ran to the bus crying so hard I could barely control my sobbing. My make-up was running, and I was shaking. I couldn't help but think no one should get this upset over a break-up. I don't remember who, but I know a friend on the school bus was talking me down as it traveled down the long country roads towards home. I prayed that my step-uncles were nowhere around when I got there. I wanted to do my chores and listen to music.

The next day we were in the hall, and Adam came up to me, and this time, I smiled. He asked me to meet him behind the stage after lunch, and I didn't fight his advances. I was heartbroken, and I would do anything to make the pain in my chest stop.

However, I learned that pain can get worse! I ran down the hall and grabbed my friend as I walked into the bathroom. I looked her in the eyes with tears rolling down my face and said Adam had his penis in his hand when I walked behind the stage. She couldn't believe the nerve of this creep. He actually thought I would give him oral sex! To be honest, I didn't even know the proper name for it at the time, but I knew right then that he was just like my uncles!

All my dreams and excitement had been crushed, so I did what I always do when I get hurt. I cut my hair and told my mother about my dad and his girlfriend. I hated all men and wanted my mom to know why. This was when things went from bad to worse. My parents decided to separate, so we were alone on the farm.

Flashback: I remember walking in, and my mother was in tears. She had a pill bottle in her hand, and I took it from her. I remember being so scared. I didn't want my mom to die. I couldn't understand why dad was doing this.

My parent's separation caused my mother to fall apart. However, it wasn't long until my mom bounced back into reality. She got a new job, so she called her brother, and we moved to Cookeville. I would not see my friends again for years.

I didn't mind the move because I was glad to leave Sparta! No one would be touching me! It wasn't long after we moved to Cookeville that my step-uncles stripped our double-wide, and it blew up in a gas explosion. To this day, the police around here never questioned what happened.

Flash-forward: I do not remember the date, but at one point, my mother and I took pictures to the detectives in Sparta, which proved that my uncles, dad, and grandparents had involvement in the double-wide explosion. Nothing was ever done.

Starting a new school also meant new boys. When I met Jax, who would be my first love, sparks lite, up inside of me. Moving to Cookeville was going to be great, or so I thought. I also met the fathers of my first two Children Jake and Troy.

The school was huge, and the girls were jealous. I was getting too much attention, so I fell into a depression. Jax would get onto me, but I would pull handfuls of my hair out. The feeling of pain gave me a release. It made Jax angry. He did not want me talking to Jake or Troy, and he did not want me to pull my hair out. I didn't want to be treated like a child, so I would do things to hurt Jax. I feel awful about it now, but at the time, I saw his love as a form of control.

Flashback: I cannot remember how, but I met a man named James, but I remember what he did to me. He was much older than me, and I think he might have lived around us on Jere Whitson. He was very pushy, and before long, he was doing things that my step-uncles did to me. I was left home alone when my mom worked, so I felt like fresh meat to the neighborhood. One night, I told my aunt about James, and she went off the deep end.

I never seen or even heard about James again until years later when he walked my cousin down the aisle at her wedding. I had already decided not to attend the wedding because I suspected that James would be attending. See years ago, my aunt had gotten back together with James's father, so he was now my cousin's step-brother. That is when I realized why she demanded that I not see James anymore. It all came together like a perfect puzzle.

After the wedding, I seen a picture on Facebook and instantly knew it was James. I have my suspicions that he too should have gone to jail because I was thirteen years old when he put his hands and mouth on me.

Flashback: I awoke from a deep sleep with a strong urge to urinate. My foot was asleep, so I tried hitting it on the floor to wake it up. A few weeks later, my foot started to turn black, so my dad's new girlfriend took me to the hospital. It was broke, and I needed a cast.

As you can see, my life was anything but ordinary. It looked one way to my parents, one way to the world, but inside of me, turmoil was brewing. I had an amazing boyfriend at school, but grown men chased after me. I wasn't being beaten any more, and I was away from my step-uncles. However, the demons were stirring.

I tried to keep my focus on my little sister because I never wanted her to be hurt the way I was as a child. My mom was working, and at home, I would cook dinner and take care of the chores.

I don't know how I managed to learn anything in school since I had a horror film/soap opera playing out in my life behind the curtain. I was an actress, playing my starring role, and my playwright was in bed with Satan. However, my story would never see Broadway as it was much too risqué.

**White County Middle School
In its glory day before it was demolished.**

Tina Louise Kirby 1990
Cookeville Middle School

Flash-Forward: Jax is still in love with me after all these years. My heart hurts for him because we were both robbed of our youth. Out of everyone in my life, he has offered me a place to live with no expectations, except that I am myself. He sees the young girl hiding behind my pain, and he wants me to come back to life. Maybe one day I will. Jax is also disabled, and we have the same neurologist.

I need a break. Life is fixing to get worse.

CHAPTER FOURTEEN
"8th Grade"
Fourteenth year of my Life
"The mental hospital"

1991 and the Hubble Telescope

Launched into space, and Roseanne was playing on ABC. Still, 1991 brought me great sadness. I only found one picture of me this year. My parents got back together, and we moved into the big white house on the corner of Willow and west 7th street in Cookeville, Tennessee.

I loved having a bedroom upstairs because I had privacy, and I could dance. However, with every bright day comes a thunderstorm.

Flashback: my father was beating me with a bag of ice and kicking me down the hallway because I was caught on the phone with Troy.

This flashback turned my life upside down. I had bruises all over my body, so I was thrown into the custody of Children's Services. I went into foster care, which landed me in a mental hospital in Chattanooga. I had to leave Jax and the few friends I had made. I was so depressed that I tried to cut myself, and that meant I had to be sent off like a kid who broke the law. I was devastated. Troy was in and out of my life. So much so that my memories are random.

Flashback: Troy was a DJ at one of the local radio stations, and I loved music. One time my friend took me over to Troy's trailer, and he was watching porn. The one thing that I remember is that Troy would not leave me alone. He once sent me Oreo's to my school with flowers and dropped letters down the grate to my basement window when we lived on Jere Whitson.

I was told that I had made plans to run off with Troy, which is why DCS sent me off, but I was cutting my arms, and I wanted to die. Everything I loved was gone, and I had been forced to live with strangers.

Flash-Forward: Jax is convinced that it was he and I that made plans to run off. I have recently spoken with his mother that makes me believe that it was Jax that I wanted to run off with. Jax and I had a strong friendship. I have a suspicion that I made plans to leave the school with Jax, but that is only a theory.

Flashback: I am in the mall in Chattanooga, and my DCS worker is buying me a Motley Crue CD.

Yes, my DCS worker needed to buy pipe tobacco, so we went to the mall before she took me to the mental hospital. I had never explored music before, but I loved the song "Kickstart my Heart." So, Dr. Feelgood would get me through many days of depression.

While in Moccasin Bend, I met Ace, and he was a boy that I grew attached to, but I was scared of him. He would beat his head against the wall if he weren't allowed to talk to me when he wanted to. I was moved from Smallwood to Pinebreeze during my stay at the hospital. I won't lie; I had some sense of safety while living there because no one could hit me.

I remember going on different outings into the woods and making clay pots in the ground. I do not recall anyone's name from my time here, but I do remember that a few of the staff members were weird. I remember one of them telling us that she was once a patient in the "main hospital." I think it was an attempt to scare us, but I only yearned to get my hands on a cigarette.

Something just came to mind while writing this chapter. God wasn't in my life over the past few years. There were no prayers. No one went to church, nor did they speak about religion. It was indeed a total disconnection from the life I once lived.

Flashback: I was attending a meeting at the Kingdom Hall with a foster parent who was a Jehovah's Witness. Apparently, I spoke to a boy in the hallway, and it was forbidden, so I did not get to go back to the meetings.

Arial View of Moccasin Bend Mental Facility

Cookeville Junior High School

COOKEVILLE, TENNESSEE

Cecil Allen, Principal
Ron Chambers, Assistant Principal
Lester Prichard, Assistant Principal

Term and Annual Report
of

Tina Kirby

Card No. _____ Grade _8_

19 _91_ - 19 _92_

CHAPTER FIFTEEN
"9th Grade"
Fifteenth Year of my Life
"A Summer to Remember"

1992 and Bill Clinton is elected president, and Hurricane Andrew hit Florida, leaving billions in damages. I was starting the ninth grade! I was out of the mental hospital, and my parents put me in the Algood School. My dad was driving a school bus, so it was just easier for him if I went to a school on his route.

Life felt mundane for a few months, and then things went crazy.

At only 14 years old, I was an act of nature. Nothing could have prepared me for Kirk. He had long, beautiful hair, and he was shy, tall, and handsome. He loved metal music, and I was starting to venture into different types of music. All it took was one smile and his ever-famous "what" to change my life forever.

One day on the school bus, I sat next to him, and kids were throwing paper balls. One just happened to land in my lap, and I told him to grab it. This would be the beginning of the best six months of my life. I was filled with so much happiness as I spent every moment I was allowed with Kirk.

My parents were dating new people, so I was the new babysitter. Going to school and tending to my sister became routine, but Kirk made it bearable. On the weekends that my sister would go to my dad's, my mom and I would take a trip to Georgia, and Kirk would always go.

I had no idea that he was a virgin, but soon I would discover this on the bathroom floor in a small apartment in Ringgold, Georgia. We made love on the floor, the bathtub, and basically anywhere we could. Our make-out sessions got so intense that I craved him all the time. He was a fantastic lover and friend. With Kirk, I could be curious, and I felt safe to explore my body and his without feeling insecure.

I felt like a virgin with Kirk. I got to choose, and it wasn't dirty or forced. It was so natural and kind. Kirk was a gentle soul, even if he looked like a bad boy. There was nothing dangerous about him, and I loved every moment that we were together.

It wasn't just the sex either. Kirk had a way of making me feel loved. From the way, he looked at me to the way he touched my face. It was a full circle of happiness. My love for metal music grew, and it fueled our lovemaking, like pouring gas on a fire.

My father would change the course of my life forever. My father gave Kirk an ultimatum. He wanted Kirk to marry me, but Kirk was terrified. I would not learn of this until 2017. It has caused me great pain, but it also brought about the closure I needed.

1992 was also the year that my parents charged me with unruly through Putnam County Juvenile court. It set the events that would kill me in motion. I don't mean like physical death, but in all aspects, I did not exist anymore. I was a shell. I felt almost robotic. I went along with everything I was told to do. I didn't question anyone.

Some people change, some stay the same, but true love while it may go dormant never dies! Tina Milligan - 2019

CHAPTER SIXTEEN
"10th Grade"
Sixteenth Year of my Life
"Marriage & Divorce"

1993 and an idiot drove a bomb into the World Trade Center, and Meatloaf sings the number one hit "I would do anything for love (But I won't do that)."

Kirk and I were not speaking, and for the life of me, I cannot bring the memory to focus. However, it set in motion something I never saw coming. During this time, I had started talking to Troy again because I knew he could get me cigarettes.

My parents did not approve so unbeknownst to me; my dad began recording my phone conversations. I had made plans to sneak out of my bedroom and meet Troy late one night. My dad knew about the meeting, and he was setting Troy up to be arrested, but we changed the time at the last moment, so I made it out of the apartment without anyone knowing.

My parents were divorced now, so I had been living with my dad. He had a fight with his new girlfriend, so he rented a small apartment for us. In almost every way possible, I was my dad's wife. I went to school, cooked and cleaned while he worked, so when Troy offered me a chance to get out of the apartment, I did not hesitate.

The fun had just begun, and I took a hard drag off my Salem cigarette when Blue lights stopped me in my tracks. I actually think I dropped the cigarette. So, there we were.... going to jail. I was terrified and did not know what to do.

Troy was born in 1972, so he was roughly five and a half years older than me. After the arrest, everything started moving faster than the speed of light. From being interrogated by the Cookeville PD to signing the marriage certificate, it feels like it all happened in mere seconds. I was 15 and married to a man I didn't really even know.

I started my first job at Dairy Queen on Spring Street in Cookeville, Tennessee, shortly after I said: "I do." I never broke up with Kirk, and things spiraled out of control so fast. I was now living in the adult world, wondering how did I get here, and how can I go back?

I should have been excited for my Sweet 16, but it only continued to be more heartache. I tried to tell Troy that I loved Kirk, but he wouldn't listen. When I went back to school, I saw Jax, and I knew I had broken his heart. Little did he know it wasn't my marriage to Troy that changed my heart, no, it was a summer with Kirk.

I am not trying to bad mouth anyone in this book, but Troy always made it out like I hurt him on purpose. When that didn't work, he would play on my immaturity and ignorance. Troy was too old for me, and I had no real romantic feelings for him.

I was a trophy to Troy, and if he tells you anything different, then ask him about the calendar books, he kept with all his fornication proudly documented. He was a smooth talker, and he had been blessed with large genitalia, but he was an egotistical jerk. Troy, he could manipulate his way out of anything. My grandmother called him a degenerate and a con-artist.

I had some fun going to concerts, but it's all a blur. I remember alcohol, sex, school, and work. That was my life. I was a kid trying to "fake it till you make it" and I wasn't faking it very well. I have never been one to lie or hide my feelings about the person I love, so I couldn't play the part for very long without the truth coming out. I am a good actress, but when it comes to matters of the heart, my game is lousy.

I met Mr. & Mrs. Smith this year. Their son worked with Troy, so we all became friends. They turned out to be like second parents. I will always have love in my heart for them as they didn't have to be there for me. I wasn't their child or responsibility, but they always answered when I called. I put them through so much, but they still had unconditional love for me. Even now, if I were hungry or homeless, I could call them for help. They knew how badly I loved my parents and wanted a healthy relationship with them, but at this time in my life, that wasn't possible.

Flash-forward: Today is April 10, 2019, and I am back to editing my book. Coffee, Ice Water, and sour Gummy Worms are keeping me focused.

Before the marriage, my new step-mom Jan tried to get me into pageants, but I wasn't really in the mood. I was a country girl, so I wanted a four-wheeler and open land. I hated dresses!

I felt so uncomfortable in this dress.

CHAPTER SEVENTEEN
"11th Grade"
Seventeenth Year of my life
"Longing for him"

1994 and 350,000 people show up to Woodstock, and Lion King hits the Big Screen. I thought being married was awful, and I found myself cheating all the time with every boy that had always wanted me. HAHAHA, that's what Troy wanted everyone to think, but that is not how it all happened.

When I came back to Cookeville, every boy I had ever liked wanted me, but I was married. Being the forbidden fruit wasn't fun, especially when I was the only person left hurting after the party was over. Kirk was in my every thought, but I broke his heart when I married Troy.

I was rebelling, and I didn't care who knew. I wanted out! I wanted Kirk, but he didn't want me. I tried everything to get Troy to divorce me, but nothing seemed to work. During this time, I had a few sexual partners, but it was nothing like Troy thought.

I worked with a guy at Shoney's, and after my manager slipped me energy pills, I ended up in the bed of a boy I didn't even know. There was also an older man that Troy let live in our Duplex. I am ashamed to say it, but I don't even remember the men's names. These sexual encounters happened once, and then I moved on because I only had sex with them out of rage. It was anger, teenage hormones, and alcohol that fueled my transgressions.

Things always seem to go from bad to worse when sex is involved. Troy was gone all the time. I was left at home alone, and while most young wives would have picked up a book, I started calling the sex phone lines. It was a sad attempt to have a conversation with someone. Troy was working at the bars and having a good time while I sat in a 30 x 20 studio apartment. I felt so alone, and the worse it got, the more I looked for a way to numb the pain.

Unlike my friends, at this age, I didn't turn to alcohol or drugs. No, sex was my addiction and rage-fueled my erotic behavior. It was dangerous and risky, but I wanted to feel something, and no matter what I tried, I couldn't feel anything. I was empty, and nothing I tried could bring genuine emotions other than anger.

The third sexual encounter was with a longtime friend from high school. I cried when I left his house because I destroyed a beautiful friendship. If you are reading this, please know that I am so sorry. You were my BFF in High School!!

The rage turned to depression, which slowly turned into suicide, so Troy had me put in a mental hospital for a while. Then he took me to the DA in an attempt to charge me with adultery. That is where I met Patrick. He was a wild boy, but he understood me. We both loved other people, but we also had physical needs screaming like a volcano fixing to erupt. So, I relived my favorite memory. Making love on the side of the bathtub with Kirk. Yes, I possibly needed mental health services, because now I was living out my fantasies. I was playing pretend with a living, breathing alternate man.

I have to thank God for my grandma Abigail. She got wind of what was going on and somehow talked Troy into bringing me for a visit. She grounded me in ways that only a grandma can calm a person. She knew things without me speaking, and her hugs could make everything right in the world.

At some point during the trip to California, I decided to make peace with the past. I was going to try to make my marriage work. I now know that my demons were only sleeping.

I do not remember much talk about my dad or religion during this time of my life. I think I still harbored a great deal of anger towards my father, and it was something I could not talk about with my grandma. I was enjoying her smiles far too much to make her sad.

Flashback: We are sitting in the bedroom of the upstairs apartment playing strip poker with one of Troy's friends and my friend Rhonda.

It is tough to write about this because we lost Rhonda to cancer a few years ago. For a short period, after I got married, she was a good friend, but the drugs took over her life.

These pictures are of when I saw Little Texas in concert and my visit to see Grandma Abigail and Grandpa Leo.

You can only beat someone down for so long before they come back fighting. – Tina Milligan 2019

CHAPTER EIGHTEEN
"12th Grade"
Eighteenth year of her life
"I am a Mom"

1995 and Oklahoma City was bombed, and we lost Orville Redenbacher. There were so many tragedies this year that I had trouble choosing two. It seems everyday people are losing loved ones due to the terrorist.

My life is about to change forever, and I didn't have any warning. Shortly after leaving the mental hospital, Mr. Smith paid for me to stay at the local Howard Johnson motel. I was basically homeless, but I had a job and a vehicle. Mr. & Mrs. Smith had helped me buy my first car, and I was making payments to them every week.

I had invited Troy, Jax, and Jake to the hotel to see me on separate occasions, and I had sex with them. I was free and could do anything I wanted, and I did. I realized on the day that I met Jake that he was not wearing protection. I pushed him off of me as I said: "Jake, I do not have birth control." At that moment, I felt it. I felt my world stop. I know it might sound crazy, but

I felt my body become pregnant. It was the weirdest sensation.

I tried to tell Jake, but he wasn't having any part of it. Troy had convinced him that I was a whore. Troy saw me as his possession, and he was going to do anything to get me back. I called Jake's mom, and she met me for coffee. She also thought I was crazy and informed me that Jake was a virgin.

Here I was sitting in a booth at Hardee's feeling like the biggest failure on earth. She asked me what I was going to do about it, and I said I am having the baby. It was the most natural response, so I got up and went home. I am sure having an abortion would have made everyone happy, but Madonna's song "Papa don't Preach" played over and over in my head. I think I talked to my baby girl all night. I apologized for my mistakes and promised that I would never leave her or make her feel the way I did right now.

Patrick had invited me to his dad's place in another town, so I took off up the interstate. I did make one stop to tell Jake that I was leaving town. I do not remember where Patrick lived, but not too long after I got there, I dropped something under the bed. That is when I saw more guns than I had ever seen in my life. I jumped in the car and headed back to Cookeville. I was horrified.

Judge Hudson had signed a truancy warrant because I was skipping school. I had just laid down to sleep at my stepmom's house when the police showed up. I went straight to the juvenile detention center. The hospital told them that I was not pregnant, so I went along with what they said. I was so numb emotionally that I didn't give it a second thought.

My mom called her lawyer and got me out of juvenile, so I went back to my dad's house and started school. Then the vomiting started, and it wasn't like normal morning sickness. I was sick, 24/7. Eventually, my stepmom bought a test, and it was bluer than the ocean. I was pregnant.

I called Troy, Jake, and Jax....but I had to make one more phone call, and it was to Kirk. Neither one of us can remember having sex around this time, but we both recall that I called him. We were hoping that he was the father. I wanted my baby to belong to Kirk, but deep down, I knew it was Jake's baby.

Troy had convinced himself that I was some kind of nymphomaniac. He wanted to see the worst in me. I had fallen into a deep depression. I didn't care what anyone thought of me. At some point during this time, I went to live with my mom in Ringgold, Georgia. I went to school there for a short period. I met a boy there named Jeremiah, who was in JROTC. He was very helpful to me, and we had sex once. I later found out that he was a virgin.

Then it happened. The first spot of Hidradenitis Suppurativa came up on my breast. My mom was worried I had cancer, so my stepdad took me to Erlanger to have it checked out. The doctors there really didn't know what it was, but I remember how painful it felt. I was terrified that I had caught some STD.

Troy came down and picked me up not long after that, and I never said goodbye to Jeremiah. My mother was so angry that she put all the pictures she had of me in the dumpster. I was hurt, but I gathered my things and went back to Cookeville.

Flashback: I went to live with my dad and grandpa down in Walling for a few weeks. It was at this time that I realized that everything in the house had been stolen from my parent's double-wide before it exploded. I know my dad had to know, but when William started coming around, I moved back to Cookeville.

Mrs. Smith had helped me get into Algood Manor Apartments. I had limited income, so I bought used furniture, and Mrs. Smith bought me a baby crib. Troy got the utilities turned on because I was a minor. He had his own apartment, so I was going to do this on my own.

I cleaned the apartment and started getting ready to be a mom. I had made friends with a neighbor, and her boyfriend was a therapist. (God sometimes sends you gifts at the most unexpected times)

Flashback: HAHAHA, she thought you could try that crap out in an apartment. Julie, I will forever laugh when I think about you trying your mace indoors!

Ok, are you ready? I went WILD! I slept with a man from work, then there was Kyle, Tommy, Ethan, Jared, a boy from Sparta, and Noah. In the summer of 1995, my pregnancy hormones were all over the place, and I was going insane.

My mom and stepdad offered me to tag along with them to Daytona Beach, and that is where I met Noah. I didn't think anyone loved me or wanted me. I was living in my car and working at the Truck Stop. I was in so much emotional pain. The only way to numb it was with sex. It was my drug of choice, and I had given it into the dealer. I knew I was good at one thing, and I perfected it every chance I got.

However, it all stopped with Noah because he talked to me. He was a biker and told me to get myself right. He said, "your baby is going to need you." Noah said, "F*** everyone else," and "you don't need them." Sometime in the middle of the night, I stole a hundred dollars from Noah, and we left Daytona. I went back to Cookeville with a different attitude.

A few weeks later, Jake took me to Big O's donuts in Cookeville. He asked for my hand in marriage, but he was just a kid, and out of fear, I said, "NO"! Troy talked me into getting back together, and I had already begun building a life with Troy's family.

The thought of losing them brought me great pain. They were the only stability that my baby would have, so I wasn't letting go. Right before my eighteenth birthday, I dropped out of High School, due to a car accident. A few days later I gave birth to Dakota! It's a Girl! However, she didn't belong to my husband. Jake was the father.

I attempted breastfeeding, but it hurt so badly. After a few days, my mom gave Dakota a bottle, so I could heal up. When my milk came in, everything went more smoothly, and she was a happy baby.

Jake and Jerry came to my apartment one night to see the baby. Jake crawled through the bedroom window and held his daughter. He knew that I was not going to leave Troy, so we decided to part ways, and I would move on with my life.

I had a perfect birth and my baby girl was healthy.

CHAPTER NINETEEN
Nineteenth Year of her life
"My son is born"

1996 and a significant snowstorm paralyzes the Midwestern United States, and I was working at McDonald's. Jake wanted a paternity test, and so I paid $700 to Cookeville Pathology. I wanted to prove that I wasn't a whore and that I knew who the father of my baby was.

Troy and I moved into a condo on 10th street, and I worked several different jobs to keep the bills paid. Troy worked and slept. He was not much help with housework or the baby. Aunt Sue started helping me more and more.

Jake and his father lived right down the road in an apartment. I heard that he had gone into the National Guard, but it wasn't long before he was sent home with a medical discharge.

One day, Jake came over to the house, and he wanted to talk about Dakota. I was not mentally prepared to see him, so the moment he kissed me, I lost all self-control. Eventually, we ended up in the shower. I felt so embarrassed because my body had changed, but he said the only loving words that he ever spoke to me. "It is ok because you had our baby. You are beautiful." That song "Here you come again" plays in my head when thinking about Jake. I can be on the path to salvation, and he would walk in and kiss me.

Troy and I were fighting because of the adultery, so he wanted to take me on a trip to California. I agreed to go. I told him that I did not want to be with him, but he insisted that I was confused.

Flashback: Troy is talking about a credit card he found at work. During the entire trip to California, he was using this credit card.

I remember the above flashback. I felt so awful after this trip and wanted to divorce Troy, but he called some men from the church over in an attempt to change my mind. He even wrote a letter to Dakota that he would change. I put it in her baby book.

The day I found out that I was pregnant with Jacob, we lost my grandpa Thomas Clarke. I could not get back for the funeral. I remember looking up at a Beverly Hill's sign from the back seat as I fell asleep crying.

Right after my nineteenth birthday, I gave birth to my second child. It's a Boy! We named him Jacob. The labor happened so fast that I barely got to the hospital. I gave birth with no pain relievers. It was an experience that I will never forget. Even though I was worried that Jake might be the father, the moment I saw Jacob, I knew he belonged to Troy.

I also knew that I would never get out of this marriage now. I was trapped, so I did the only thing I could do. We bought a house, and I accepted my life. I thought about Jake and Kirk all the time. My heart was so twisted that I could never get settled. This year the migraines started, and my legs would go numb for no reason.

I would have one anxiety attack after the other, so I kept busy with work. I had a beautiful home on Maple Avenue in Cookeville and an excellent new job at the retirement home.

I want to note here that over the past few years, Mr. & Mrs. Smith tried very hard to keep me in church and keep me grounded. Emotionally, I was unstable when it came to men. In every other part of my life, I was healthy. I cooked, clean, worked and loved my children.

Very few people knew about the battle that was going on inside of me. I was an actress, and I played my part. My heart hurt so bad that I figured it would never be right.

Trip to California & Las Vegas in 1996.

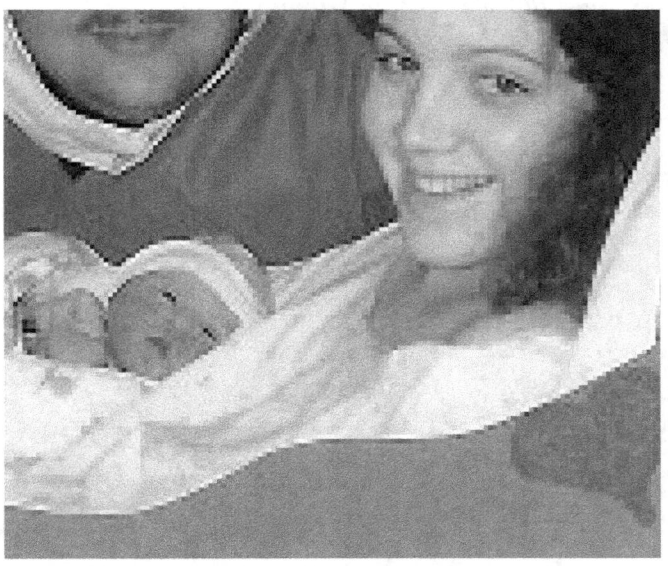

The Birth of my Son! December 1996

Being a mother was the greatest gift that God ever gave me. I want to change many choices I made over the years, but I never regret having my children. – Tina Milligan 2019

CHAPTER TWENTY
Twentieth Year of my Life
"Maple Avenue"

1997 and Diana Princess of Wales died in a car crash, and Titanic hits the big screen. I lived on Maple Avenue in Cookeville, Tennessee, and I thought life would finally settle down, but my husband continued to get himself involved in White Collar crimes. I hated him more and more.

I tried to talk to Jake, but he was off living life. I turned to the internet for social interaction, and I found "Love City Chat." On this chat, I made friends with a girl in Canada. Her name was Jade, and I did everything I could to bring her to visit me in the states. When she came to visit, I introduced her to Kirk.

I figured one of us should be happy, but I was WRONG. You cannot get over the love of your life by hooking him up with other women. It doesn't work. You are still going to want him. No matter how many men you bring into your life, no one will ever be "THE ONE."

After a few months, Jade had to go back to Canada. I think Kirk broke up with Jade because he started calling me more often. It wasn't long before I was praying that I could be back with Kirk.

Kirk and I had been talking for a few weeks. He had even come by for breakfast a few times. Then the day came that changed my feelings towards Kirk. Kirk and I were sitting on the couch, and we starting kissing. All the old feelings were still there, and it wasn't long before I was giving him oral sex.

After Kirk left, I went into a state of depression. I felt used by the one man that I had always loved. He had changed, and he was so different from the young boy that I dated in 1992. I felt like sex was meaningless to him. It was cold and just for self-gratification. What had gone wrong? Kirk now acted about sex the way I used to, and that is a dangerous place to be!

Troy's mom was babysitting the kids, so I threw myself into work to numb the pain. It was a hot mess and more broken. I decided to get a divorce, and I would live alone and never date again. I could not handle relationships. I wasn't good at it! My heartfelt tainted to the point of no return, or so I thought.

Flashback: I am standing in front of a Christmas tree, and my grandma Abigail was visiting us. I had the video recorder on, and my dad says, "look at that fat ass," I remember Jade being upset that my dad would say such a thing to me, especially in front of everyone. The sad thing is I didn't hear it the first time. No, I heard it when I replayed the video with my friend.

    Besides my children, the memory of my grandma visiting is one of the best from this year. It is like she knew when everything was out of control, so she would come in my life long enough to ground me. She had no idea that Troy and I were about to end our marriage, and I saw no point in upsetting everyone.

Jade & I - 1997

CHAPTER TWENTY-ONE
Twenty-First Year of my Life
"My Baby Girl is Born"

1998 and Bill Clinton is caught having an affair, and Forest Fires in Florida force 120,000 to flee their homes. I finally managed to move out and leave Troy. I could not take it anymore, and wouldn't you know it... Jake shows up at my house while I am packing. He has Edgar with him.

We were all sitting on the couch, and I didn't know Edgar, but he felt the need to introduce himself by saying, "I bet I can guess the color of your panties!" I was shocked by his comment, but I quickly realized that I have a hole between my legs. We all laughed it off, and I was three sheets to the wind, so I decided to take a shower.

In the middle of washing my hair, Jake jumps in the shower, and he is naked. Yep. You guessed it. "Here you come again" is playing in the background. At the same speed as his ejaculation, Jake was gone. I was once again left hurt and used. Later, Edgar called me and apologized for Jake's behavior, but I was just disgusted with myself. I had come too far to let Jake drag me down again.

My landlord helped me get moved back into Algood Manor, and little did I know that Sara would be living right next door to me. She shared my phone and her knowledge of single men in the area.

Seth worked at a local car dealership, and he was raising his daughter. We hit it off well, but after one night at his house, I knew that I had to stop this before it started. I felt dead inside. He was a good man, and was not fit to be anyone's wife. I still loved Kirk, and I thought it would be best if I stuck to being a mom.

Now I know why Mrs. Smith called me the Taz. It was from the Tasmanian Devil Cartoon. I could screw up my life in seconds, and I wasn't about to take anyone else with me. I even thought about allowing Troy's parents to adopt my children because I felt like the worse mother on the planet. I knew my kids would grow up to hate me if they ever knew the truth about me.

Well, a few weeks before Valentine's Day, I ended up on a three-way phone conversation. Edgar and Sara had planned all this out. Edgar heard me say that I would date him if he asked me out. A few minutes later,

Edgar showed up at my door. He brought me cigarettes, and he didn't leave. His behavior was something new. He cooked, cleaned, helped with the kids, and bought me things with the money he had earned. I was in heaven. All thoughts of Kirk and Jake disappeared when Edgar came into my life. My dad and I had started to talk again, and he had remarried again to a nice woman named Tammy.

It wasn't long, and I was pregnant with my third child. I had to work, plan a wedding for June, finish my divorce, and try to relax. I was sick all the time, and I didn't have the energy to do anything. My new stepmom and I bonded during the wedding planning. We made a school bus cake together, which we traded for the limousine for my wedding. She brought sunshine into my life, and slowly I let her in. I wondered if she would ever leave.

Fast Forward: Tammy is still married to my dad. Today is April 10, 2019, last Monday, Tammy was the first to read this book in its entirety. I will talk about this more later on but, it ended badly. I moved out of my parent's rental house and left the mountain, never to return. If you learn anything from this, please do not trust people who have been lied to. I assumed that she knew the whole truth. My dad had sugar-coated and lied to everyone, even his wife.

My grandparents were going to be at my wedding, and everything was going great... until it wasn't. My step-sister's boyfriend went out with Edgar the night before the wedding because he was his best man. They show up at the wedding, and I am pregnant in my wedding dress as my world comes crashing down.

My mom comes in and tells me that Edgar had told his best man, "That he had never been faithful to any woman and didn't know if he could be faithful to me." I ran out of the venue and drove back to my parents'. I ripped the dress off and cried, it was all over, and I had hit an all-time new low.

Of course, you know me. I am full of empathy and guilt from my transgressions, so I took Edgar back, and we got married on my parent's front porch six days later. He begged my forgiveness, and I accepted his apology.

During my pregnancy, we lived in Algood, Baxter, Sparta, Georgia, Chattanooga, and Cookeville. I think most people would find this year to be pure insanity, but I continued fighting the good fight in my attempt to make a life for my children. We were even homeless at one point, and we had to stay with Troy. That didn't last long because Jacob came down the hallway carrying a porn magazine that he found under Troy's bed.

We went to the homeless shelter, and then we moved back to Algood Manor Apartments. I will never forget this Thanksgiving as the grocery store in Algood gave me a grocery cart full of food.

Edgar was on probation and continued to have problems with the court. I found myself on my pregnant knees, begging God for help. The church paid Edgar's court fees, and we got ready for the baby.

It's a Girl! Another December baby, and by this time, you might think I planned this, but it always seemed to happen that I gave birth in December. We named her Morgan. I was in love. Morgan would be my last child, and I was going to spoil her rotten.

The doctor found precancerous cells on my cervix while I was pregnant, so I got my tubes tied. No more babies, and no more running around. I was finally settled, so I took a job with the state, and we moved into a lovely house on Sixth Street in Cookeville.

People say bad things come in three's, but I happen to think that my blessings come in three's. Dakota, Jacob, and Morgan saved me in so many ways. They are my heart and the reason I fight to stay alive. – Tina Milligan 2019

COFFEE BREAK

CHAPTER TWENTY-TWO
Twenty-Second year of my Life
"Moving"

1999 and I went to work at Pacesetters.

Edgar worked for Smith Electric. For a few months, we had a picture-perfect life. We took vacations and visited my grandparents in Florida. I was making good money, and my babies were happy.

Then, things started to change. I was working all the time, and Edgar was home alone with the kids. I felt that things were spinning out of control.

We decided to move from the sixth street house to Carolina Avenue. Then, we ended up moving to Nashville, Gleason, Dresden, and then Sidonia. With every move, life got worse and worse for me. I attempted suicide and nearly succeeded. So, Edgar put me in a mental hospital for a few days, and I cleared my head. At this point, I think he even tried to take the kids away from me, but I put my foot down.

See, I was far away from home. I had no one, and we lived near David's ex-wife. She was very flirtatious, and because I once behaved like her, I knew all the signs were there for this to end badly. Edgar had got hurt at work, and he started taking pain medication. He became hateful and mean. I was working full-time, taking care of my mother-in-law, and dealing with Edgar.

So, what did I do? I started calling Troy and Jake. They were the only people that I felt I could talk to when my life was falling apart. Of course, Troy told me I deserved it because I cheated on him, and Jake was living his life and wanted no part of mine. Everyone wanted to take my children and forget about me.

We were living in a dump in Sidonia. I passed my ASVAB and signed to go into the Army, but I couldn't go. Jake's mother had threatened to take my daughter if I left her with Edgar. I wanted to move Edgar back to Cookeville with the kids and go to basic training, but my dreams again were crushed because of my ignorance.

I didn't realize that Jake's mom couldn't take Dakota away from Edgar. I had a good plan for my family. My grandmother Abigail said it would help me get my mind straight, and I would always be able to provide for my family.

I took my children and headed to Georgia. I could not bear living with Edgar anymore. I was afraid of everything, but I was mostly scared that I would lose my children. They were my life. They were the reason I didn't give up.

I can only find a few pictures from this year. Edgar told me it was because our computer crashed and I lost thousands of photos. The year ended on a sad note as my mom's dad had passed away on December 12, 1999.

CHAPTER TWENTY-THREE
Twenty-Third Year of my Life
"College"

2000 and two devastating earthquakes kill 14,000 people in Turkey, and an F5 tornado touches down in Oklahoma City, Oklahoma, killing 38 people. I knew I was the only one that could change my life. I felt Satan on my back, so I tried to do little things, so he wouldn't notice.

I got my GED 02/08/2000. I left Edgar and moved to Trenton, Georgia, to be close to my mother. The marriage was on the rocks, and Edgar was abusing pain medication.

It wasn't long before I had to leave my mother's house because she slapped my daughter in the face. It brought back so many awful memories of her hitting me as a kid, so I went to the church, and they helped me find a place to live.

I went to work for Shaw Industries and waited on Edgar to straighten up. Then one day, I got my tax return and went to Sidonia and gave him a choice. He loaded up everything, and Edgar went back to Trenton with me to start working for Shaw Industries.

We were working all the time. Our paychecks were big, and we could buy our kids clothes and nutritious food to eat! The long hours at work and lack of proper childcare made it so hard to keep working all the overtime.

I started giving plasma to get extra money for groceries. I was burning the candle at both ends, and so I decided to apply to a college in Cookeville.

My dreams came true the day I opened the letter from Tennessee Technological University. I got accepted into college! I found a house and moved my family back to Cookeville. I was on cloud nine, and nothing was going to stop me from becoming the woman I always wanted to be.

I was working three different jobs and going to college. Edgar was the primary caregiver for the children, but I always had breakfast with them. This year was perfect. We were living in family housing on campus, and I was coming to life.

College life was remarkable, and I made friends. It was the first time that people laughed at my jokes. Then, Edgar moved in with a coworker from the plant he was working at in Gainesboro. We eventually worked things out, but Satan was pulling a shuck and jive.

College years were some of the best years of my life.

CHAPTER TWENTY-FOUR
Twenty-Fourth Year of my Life
"Lies & Cancer"

2001 and the twin towers are hit by the terrorist. I remember being in a study lab on campus when the news came on. It was unbelievable that the USA was under attack. I felt so scared, and all I wanted was my babies in my arms. I picked them up from daycare and headed to our house.

I remember getting the mail, and my heart dropped. Jake was asking for more DNA tests before he would pay child support. I was on public assistance while I was in college, but this would mean I would have to go back to work.

I was outraged because Jake knew that I had already worked hard to pay for DNA testing. He actually thought I had tampered with the first test, so he asked for one through the court. Jake didn't care about my children or me. He wanted a way out of the obligation. Edgar decided that we needed to move, so we left Cookeville.

We settled in a small trailer in Gainesboro, Tennessee, to get away from the stress in Cookeville. In

Gainesboro, elementary schools were more modest, but the drive was no fun. I did like the fact that everyday life became more peaceful in Jackson County.

Flash Forward: I found out years later that Jake's mothers' family were all from Jackson County. So, there was someone always reporting back to Jake about my life. He wanted me to think that he didn't know, but he knew more than I ever imagined.

Edgar went to work, so we could pay our bills on time! On September 11, 2001, when the twin towers got hit by airplanes. I was sitting in my classroom at TTU. The entire nation fell to their knees in prayer as it was the terrifying time in history. I felt how much the terrorist hate American, and it scared me to death!

The rest of this year was spent with me clinging to my family because of depression. Everyone around me seemed very melancholy and distant. I was feeling very sick and bleeding all the time. We moved back to Carolina Avenue, and I was a stay at home, mom.

Dr. Grey said I had an ovarian cyst, but I decided to get a second opinion. I had surgery on Halloween of this year to relieve some pain, and we spent Christmas with my grandma in Florida. She was battling cancer, and I missed her terribly.

While we were in Florida, we talked about moving there, so I could be close to my grandma Abigail. However, public school was not an option, and we could not afford private school.

Flashback: Jake calls me and tells me that his wife had died from cancer. I find out that he lied to me, and it brought back all the old feelings of distrust.

The above memory was probably the worst thing Jake ever did besides abandon his daughter. My grandma was fighting cancer, and his lies made no sense to me. He only wanted to hurt me, and I still do not understand why.

CHAPTER TWENTY-FIVE
Twenty-Fifth Year of my Life
"Hysterectomy"

2002 and I became very sick and had to undergo a full hysterectomy in March. There were no other options since I had cancer and endometriosis. I had already gone through surgery last October, but now they were taking my ovaries and uterus. I didn't talk to anyone about it, because I was scared, and I had adopted the "get er done attitude."

On top of that, I had to comply with the court order and take my children for DNA testing. Since I was sick again, I had to seek public assistance, and that meant I had to go after Troy and Jake for child-support.

We were living in a beautiful house on Ensor Drive. Our family life seems to be coming together, and I loved being home with my babies. However, shortly after my surgery, I started having unhealthy thoughts about ending my life.

Edgar had been out of town on a business trip, so I went to the mood disorder unit at the hospital in

Lebanon, Tennessee. It was a lovely place, and I got tons of much-needed rest. The doctors were amazing. They did a few tests to determine that I needed to be on hormones because I was going through surgical menopause. It was so terrifying because I felt like a different person.

Flashback: I am standing in the courtroom, and the judge reads off the test results. He says without a pause, "I guess Mrs. Milligan knows who the fathers of her children are."

I wanted to laugh, but I was playing a part while hiding the fact that cancer had just stolen all my lady parts out of my body. I did not want Troy or Jake to see me weak. They had already tried to paint me as a mentally unstable mother. My walls were up, and I had on my poker face. Troy's step-father had come to court with me to verify that I had held 2-3 jobs at the same time since I was 15 years old. I wasn't a bum; no, I was recovering from major surgery.

While we were living on Carolina Avenue, I got an overnight envelope from Disney World saying I had won a vacation through the Minute Maid Company. I was so happy because I needed a way from Cookeville, and I always wanted to take my children to Disney

World. Poor Dakota was sick the entire trip, but we made the best out of it.

     My usual reaction to most things is to freak out, cry, call someone for advice, pray while taking a shower, and then do something about it. I wasn't a quitter. There have been times that I wanted to die, but after my meltdown, I always got back up and tried to do better. Ms. Lewald said I was a very resilient person. I think again now, it was the only way that I knew to survive. It was either that or death, and I always chose life for my children. I knew they needed me.

My Family

CHAPTER TWENTY-SIX
Twenty-Sixth Year of my Life
"Rainbow City"

2003 and Space Shuttle Columbia exploded, killing seven people. I remember I just stood at the television and cried. How could this happen? I didn't understand, so I watched the news off and on for days until I learned that a known problem with a piece of foam caused the crash. Something so simple that could have been fixed was left unattended, and people died.

We started out this year living on Carolina Avenue. I didn't know it, but Edgar was back to abusing narcotics. We had been in marriage counseling, and I felt that Edgar had been cheating. He had been going out of town for meetings. His friends/co-workers enjoyed drinking and going to strip clubs. I could not handle it anymore, so I started going through his clothing, dresser drawers, and bags.

One night, I went through his memory discs from his computer and found images of other women. I confronted him when he got home, and we got into a huge argument. Somehow during the discussion, he shut my foot in the door, so the police were called. He moved out, and I fell apart.

A few weeks later, we got back together, and Edgar quit his job. He worked for a man for a short time, but the guy he worked for had a bad drug problem, and it made things at home even more complicated.

That is when Edgar decided to move us to Rainbow City, Alabama. I didn't want to go, but Edgar gave me no choice. He said I could either come with him or stay in Cookeville. He had a good job offer in Rainbow City. This time the kids would be going to some of the best schools and living in an apartment with a swimming pool.

We started working the flea markets on the weekends, which made me miss home. I yearned to see my sister and the mountains. I mostly remember the tornado warnings while we lived there. I loved a good storm, but tornados terrified me.

It wasn't long, and my sister hit the rebellious teenage stage, and she came to live with us. I loved this time in my life. I did not feel alone with Kathy by my side. I guess it has always been that way. My sister was my best friend.

I had applied for disability because I had stage 3 Hidradenitis Suppurativa. HS is a severe skin disease that causes pockets of inflammation the hair root under the skin near your sweat glands to form. There is no cure for this condition, but many life factors like heat and stress can intensify the pain.

The very first spot of Hidradenitis Suppurativa was the place I mentioned earlier that came up on my breast when I was seventeen years old. It wasn't until my early twenties that Dr. Hamilton gave me a definite diagnosis at Vanderbilt Dermatology.

HS nodules were so unpredictable. I never knew when one would come up under my arm, in my groin, on my breast or on my buttocks. I kept bandages, and I took several showers each day.

My health continued to decline, so Edgar decided to move us to Sparta, Tennessee, and open a pet store. He was also trying to start his own wholesale business. I had a bad feeling about moving, but I decided to trust Edgar. Little did I know that our lives were going to do a 180!

2003 Carolina Avenue

Flash-Forward: It is 2019, and my cat Tigger is still with me to this day. He is my faithful friend and a love bug!

CHAPTER TWENTY-SEVEN
Twenty-Seventh Year of my Life
"Disney World"

2004 and Hurricane Jeanne kills over 3,000 people in Haiti, and The Statue of Liberty reopens to the public. To make matters worse, the CIA admits that there were no weapons of mass destruction before the 2003 invasion of Iraq.

After trying for several years to get my disability, the day finally came when it was approved. Edgar and I were living on Penny Lane with my sister and our children. Things were almost perfect until I called the school to check on my step-daughter. That is when we found out that she was in foster care.

In one week, I became an instant stepmother. DCS came over to do the home evaluation, and we were approved. There was just one little problem with that, Edgar could not go to Weakley County. He had over $5,000.00 in worthless checks there from years ago, and the judge said that if he came back to that county, he would put him in jail.

When we lived down there, Edgar was making payments on them, but now we had to pay them off. Since I had just got my disability back payment, I agreed to pay off the checks for Edgar. The day we went to pick up Jasmine, the weather was awful. I remember the cold rain hitting my face as Edgar asked me to take Jasmine to the hair salon while they were in court. She wasn't handling the situation very well because it wasn't long ago that she lost her grandmother.

Being a stepmom at a young age is probably the most horrible job as a parent. I had to pay for her parent's transgressions and most of which happened while I was still in high school. She was depressed, sad, and angry. I was the convenient punching bag, and I had no idea how to handle her behavior.

When it came to boys, I only had the knowledge that came from my mistakes and my parent's bad choices. I wasn't going to make her get married, so I decided to embrace the situation. I figured if she were with us when she saw her boyfriend, then things would be ok. I WAS WRONG, and after you let a child do something, it is harder to undo it.

Jasmine fought us on everything. Jasmine and my sister were not getting along, so life was even more complicated. Kathy went to live with our father, and that turned out to be a disaster, so she moved in with friends and ended up getting married at the courthouse during her senior year of high school.

During this time, Jasmine's mother decided to let me know that she had sex with my husband. I had a total meltdown. That woman was so jealous and cruel that she just had to make my life even harder. I was raising her child, and she was out having a good time.

I hated her, and I wanted to divorce Edgar. However, when my empathy hit, I put my children first and decided to pretend it didn't happen. After the meltdown, I got so depressed that I could not get out of bed. I had hot flashes all the time, and the HS was relentless.

Edgar started making some money, so we made plans to take the family back to Disney World for vacation. It was fun until Edgar got sick. Jasmine was allowed to bring her boyfriend on the trip, and that turned out to be another big mistake. On the upside, since we were in Florida, we did get to visit my grandma Abigail and Daytona Beach.

It wasn't long after Christmas that we decided to move again. We closed down our pet store at the Flea Market and headed to the smoky mountains.

Always get advice about raising kids from someone who raised their kids. If they didn't do such a good job, then their opinion is toxic! - Tina Milligan 2019

Hold my wine....

CHAPTER TWENTY-EIGHT
Twenty-Eighth year of my life
"Mountains"

2005 and Hurricane Katrina killed many people as she tore through the coastline of Louisiana. She also made a path for new demons to come into my life.

Moving to a cabin in the Smoky Mountains was terrific. Although my health did not improve, I was soaking in the Jacuzzi tub every day, so I did heal much quicker. I loved having coffee in the mornings while I watched the kids walk to the bus.

We made one of our biggest parenting fails during the move. We allowed Jasmine's boyfriend to move with us. His parents were going through a divorce and abusing drugs, so we felt like we should take him with us.

We had come to love him as one of our children, which turned out to be a HUGE MISTAKE! We put him in school, bought his clothing, fed him, and kept a roof over his head. Then he betrayed us.

Not long after the move, Edgar found out that his brother had cancer, and his mother had Alzheimer's. After talking it over, we decided to bring them to live with us and rent out his mom's trailer in Gleason. We certainly did not want to move there, and the doctors in Knoxville were much better for his brother's treatment.

I spent the first week of my mother-in-law living with us, sitting beside her hospital bed. She was unable to walk, and her heart was giving her problems. We had to get her set up with new physicians and get her medication refills ASAP. Edgar was taking his brother to see new doctors and finish up his chemotherapy treatments. We were so busy that I do not remember sleeping.

Now that we had Edgar's mom and brother settled, and the children were in school, he decided to work from home. We had a house full of pets since we closed down the pet store. Life was busy and crazy. It was also about the time that Jake decided to come back into my life and start trouble over child support.

Edgar's business started to fail, and the man who said he would lease us the building for the pet store backed out because of conflicts with the other owners. So, we had no choice but to sell all our reptiles and other pets to the local pet store. We didn't make any money on the deal, but it took some stress off of the family at home.

Edgar started to panic when loads of wood stopped showing up to his customers, so instead of filing bankruptcy, he wrote refund checks to them. Writing bad checks turned out to be the worst mistake of his life.

Edgar started getting arrested, and I had to make trips to Sparta and Cookeville for court. Then, it happened. Jasmine was pregnant. It was only a few weeks later than she had a miscarriage. Life went from insane to almost unbearable in our household. I had lost all respect for myself as a parent, and the guilt ate me alive.

Flash-forward: I am not going to write much about Jasmine losing the baby. It is her story to tell. I am respecting her privacy when it comes to this matter.

This year brought about new challenges. My sister wanted to come live with us, so she would be closer to college, and Edgar was facing prison time for bad checks. We briefly lived in an apartment in Gatlinburg, but then we found a house on Park Road. It was big enough for the whole family, and it felt right.

Our landlord was amazing, and we were close to the schools.

It wasn't long before Jake started causing me trouble again. I let Dakota go for a visit, and he went to the court in Knoxville to seek an Ex Parte order of protection. It was a nightmare, and I had to spend every dime we had to get a lawyer to get her back. I spent more money on attorney fees fighting Jake than he ever paid in child support.

Jake didn't care that it hurt me, his daughter, or my family unit. He was out for revenge, and to this day, I do not know why. I have theories, and over the years, Jake's mother would drop hints, pointing to the conclusion that he blamed me for everything. I have come to accept the fact that I will always be the villain in his version of the story.

In September, we lost my grandpa Leo. If you know my family, then you know he was an awesome man. I returned everything that I could to Walmart to buy a plane ticket. I had to say goodbye, and I knew my grandma had to be falling apart. However, when I got there people were going through her things, and I couldn't say anything. I was only the granddaughter. Her sons had taken control. The trip to Florida was challenging because I had to go alone.

When I returned home, Edgar decided to tell me that he was going to Louisiana to work. He thought he could pay off the bad checks, and our life would go back to normal.

While all this is going on, I am smoking two packs of cigarettes a day. I fell deeper into the depression, and I was no more than a robot. I did what had to be done and slept every chance I got.

We occasionally went to the Baptist church, but I felt I had left God. I was so angry all the time, and I felt sleepy no matter how much I slept. The HS was so bad that I had one surgery after the other.

CHAPTER TWENTY-NINE
Twenty-Ninth Year of my Life
"Pain & Park Road"

2006 and George Bush is in the White House. Twelve minors were found dead in West Virginia. This year was going to be one of the worse for me, and at the time, I had no warning or clue that my whole life was about to change.

Then Eager left for Louisiana. He took Troy with him and Jasmine's boyfriend. They told me that they were going to camp and work. Edgar had bad checks, Troy owed me tons of child support, and I needed Jasmine's boyfriend out of my hair, so I could raise my children.

I was happy when they left. I could breathe again, and I got into a routine. My brother-in-law helped me with his mother, so I had more time to spend with my children.

Jake didn't stop with his tactics to try to take Dakota from me. One day, I opened the door to the police and a search warrant. Someone had told them that I was making Methamphetamine in my basement.

Ok, let us stop right here. If you know me, if you love me, or if you hate me, it doesn't matter, but one thing you know about me is that I HATE DRUGS! Of course, the police did not find anything because I did laundry in my basement!

Edgar wired me $2,000.00, and I got an attorney. I was not going down without a fight this time. Jake told the judge that he would rather see Dakota in a foster home than to see her living with me.

I was heartbroken that a person could hate me so much. I don't know what I ever did to Jake, but he hated me. He even turned down my request for an interview.

It was during this time that the doctor told me that I had early signs of Multiple Sclerosis. I went to Louisiana and told Edgar. He wasn't much help and actually brushed it off, saying that I was ok.

I made a few trips to Louisiana, but Jake had the judge issue a restraining order, so I could not see Edgar anymore. It was a bad situation, but I tried to make the best of things. During the summer, the kids and I spent almost every day at the swimming pool or in the mountains.

I didn't want to be home, but I couldn't leave Sevier County. That is when I met Tony at the Pigeon Forge Swimming Pool. He tried to hook up with me, but I had too much on my mind.

Edgar met me once in Trenton, Georgia, for an overnight visit. He also came up and took the children to the aquarium in Chattanooga. He wanted to work out our marriage, and I think he suspected that Tony was trying to get with me. I was so numb by this point that I just went through the motions of daily life.

I filled out an application for a two-bedroom apartment, and we moved. Edgar was sending me less money, and the rent at the house was $1,200.00 a month.

I gave the girls one-bedroom, and Jacob, the other bedroom. I slept in the living room, and I put my mother-in-law's hospital bed in the dining room area. We were in tight living quarters, but it felt right. My brother-in-law moved in with his new girlfriend, and I was taking care of my mother-in-law.

I found out that Edgar was cheating on me, so I turned him in to the police. It took me going down there by myself to get his exact location because he had moved a few times. When I got home, I searched the Verizon account and got a phone number.

The lady answered the phone and confirmed that she had been having sex with my husband. Once Edgar was arrested and transported back to Tennessee, I had to get his truck and belongings in Louisiana. Everything happened so fast that I was left feeling empty.

After thinking things over, I talked to Kathy. She was going to make the trip with me. My neighbor agreed to watch the children. However, God had different plans. My tire blew out on I-40, and it almost killed me. It destroyed my van, so I didn't go to Louisiana. The neighbor picked me up at the hospital, and I went home to my babies.

Troy's step-dad bought me a nice car, but I still needed to get to Louisiana. Jasmine was living with my friend, so I didn't have any help. Edgar told me that his boss in Louisiana was stealing from FEMA, so when my dad took me to get Edgar's truck, I picked up the evidence and gave it to the FBI.

That is when I met JR and decided that since I could not go into law enforcement that I would help the FBI anonymously. JR was a special agent, and his words lit a fire inside of me. He said that I was very inquisitive, and that was a good trait to have.

I had been helping law enforcement since middle school when I joined the "Just say no club." I hated drugs and saw what they did to families. Now I had a friend who I could call with information, and he would never betray my trust. To this day, he has always taken my calls and looked out for my family and me.

Fast Forward: They diagnosed me with Multiple Sclerosis in 2017, so I decided to stop all involvement with law enforcement, but in 2018, I went to a conference on reporting human trafficking. That conference lite a fire inside of me. I am always on the lookout for suspicious behavior in my community. Human Trafficking is happening all around us. Please, if you see something, say something!

I had a few good people in my life, so I filed for divorce and started officially dating Satan, aka Tony. Yes, I call him that because he built me up only to rip me to shreds.

The grass might be greener, but the snakes are bigger! Always remember that, especially if you have children! Your innocent intentions could ruin your child's life if you don't use discernment! -Tina Milligan 2019

CHAPTER THIRTY
Thirtieth Year of my Life
"My Nightmare"

2007 and Steve Jobs announces the iPhone. My life was really healthy at this point. I was making friends and spending time with my children.

Then I met up with Tony at the city park one evening, and he took me for a ride on his motorcycle. He asked me if I was ready to move on and put Edgar behind me. It wasn't long before we started living together; he was a huge help. Tony read bedtime stories, cooked, cleaned, and worked like a mule. I was on cloud nine, and he made me feel safe and loved.

Tony made love to me in a way that I had never been made love to before. This is where my addiction came back like a hurricane. I was hurt and angry, so sex gave me a release. My drug of choice was sex, and once again, it numbed the pain left by Edgar's betrayal.

I could forget everything wrong in my life and feel happy. Every time I had sex with Tony, I felt like I was slapping Edgar in the face. I did love Tony, but I wasn't in love with him. My heart was tarnished and beyond repair.

Tony took me for rides on his motorcycle, and we just clicked. He taught me how to work on my car, manage a checking account, and how to budget bills. He took the children with him when he bought my engagement ring, and he never missed a court date.

Tony stood right beside me when I fought to get my daughter back. He was there the day Dakota came home. Tony made sure I got new eyeglasses, and that I went to the dentist.

My sister gave birth to my first nephew in March. Edgar and I got divorced. Tony and I lived in a four-bedroom brick housing, and my dad came to visit, and we cooked a big meal.

If a person could feel truly happy, then that is what I felt in June 2007. We had a beautiful wedding, and I had no clue that Tony was grooming my kids and me. DCS had done a background check on him, and the children CASA worker had cleared him.

I smiled right in the face of the devil & didn't even know it.

Flashback: I got the phone call you never want to get. My best friend's daughter drowned, on July 30, 2007. Symphony Kanayda Booker will always be in our hearts.

This is one of my favorite photos I took of her and my mother-in-law Iris. We miss you both!

The above Flashback is not my story to tell. Sara knows how heartbroken I was when her daughter passed away. We all loved her very much, and she will never be forgotten.

I got the news that Jasmine ran away from her foster home, and I almost got into trouble for letting her stay at my house. I was worried sick about that child! My skin disease was getting better, but I still made weekly flights to Miami Dermatology for the Remicade injections.

After I married Tony, we lived in a Duplex, and things continued to be peaceful. We had a great Christmas, and my step-son Andrew started visiting. Then, Tony began to show his true colors.

I would have given my life and everything I owned to undo 2007. I had no idea that I was about to be destroyed. I am speaking to all single parents when I say that you must get to know someone before you allow them around your children!

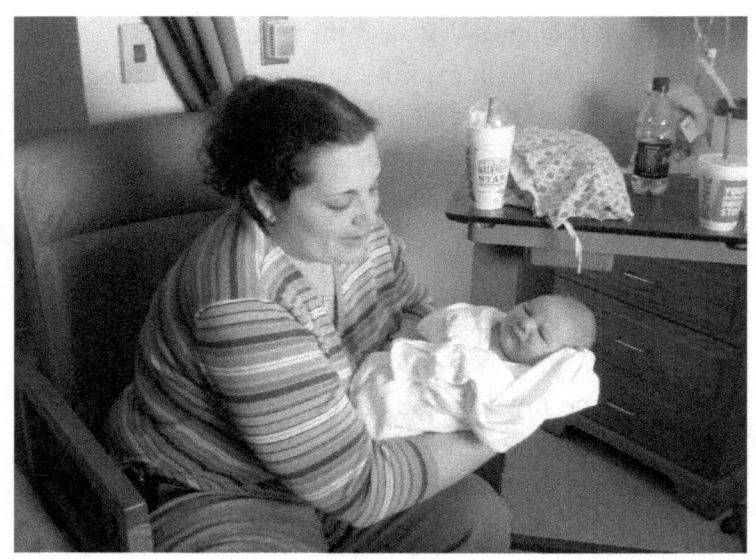

The day I became Auntie Tina.

CHAPTER THIRTY-ONE
Thirty-First Year of my Life
"Panther Creek"

2008 and we had the deadliest tornado outbreak that the United States had ever seen, and the economy hit rock bottom. My life was fixing to also hit rock bottom. I have never known pain like this before.

I decided to take the children to visit Edgar at the prison. At first, things were ok, but little by little, I fell back in love with Edger. I didn't want to, but I was weak, and he knew what to say to me. My empathy kicked in, and my problems with Tony were upon the horizon.

Tony's grandparents gave us some land, and we were clearing it off for a house. The kids were excited, and life seemed to be normal.

On February 7, 2008, my brother-in-law passed away. I had to handle his funeral alone because Edgar was in prison. Depression took over my life again, and I felt like a robot. (I know I say "Robot" many times throughout my writing, but it is true. I loved my kids, cooked, cleaned, and paid bills while I was dead inside.)

I took care of the kids and the house, but I had exited the building.

Taking my mother-in-law to a funeral, she would never remember killed me. She had started to have seizures, so she was now living in a nursing home. I was so angry with Edgar because this was all his fault. He was the reason that our fairytale ended. All the old pain came knocking at the backdoor.

My dear brother-in-law had left life insurance with strict instructions. I was to buy a house for the children that no one could ever take away from them. So, Tony and I bought a mobile home and had it put on the land his grandparents gave us.

We were able to have animals, go to the sale barn, and we even bought Dakota a horse. We had chickens, fresh eggs, and Jacob got a four-wheeler. Granny taught me how to cook like a real mountain woman, and we planted big gardens. We learned about nature, plants, and how to make money off the land.

Slowly I was coming back to life. Jacob was already driving, and he was ten years old. He was always working on something with Tony. He now had a brother too, because Tony's son came to visit more, now that we had a permanent home.

Tony adopted Dakota, and we settled into life on Panther Creek. Then lighting decided to strike us twice. On June 22, 2008, we got the news that Ma had passed away. The children were on vacation, and so I handled the entire funeral alone. Tony's granny and grandpa came with me to the funeral home, and we made arrangements to have her body sent to Michigan.

On July 22, 2008, we were camping in Hot Springs, North Carolina. I tried to call my uncle in Monterey because I had missed my regular call with him that week. He did not answer. A few days later, my other uncle found him dead. I was so numb that I thought everyone was going to die soon. I was having one surgery after the other for the HS. I was miserable, and the depression got much worse. I felt so small.

I did manage to find one picture of my uncle smiling, and he was in his wheelchair, and my children were standing on each side of him. I blew it up into an 8 x 10, and they used it for the funeral.

CHAPTER THIRTY-TWO
Thirty-Second Year in my Life
"The Devil is real"

2009 and we now land planes in the Hudson River. Seriously this happened! No one died, but it will be talked about for years to come.

I got the results back from my pap smear, and the doctor had called to ask me to come in. I felt a panic in my chest. I cut all my hair off before even going to the doctor. I just knew it was cancer again, and I was going to get myself mentally prepared.

I struggled with depression so much that I lost touch with the world around me. It felt like I was standing still, and everyone else was happily enjoying life while I was frozen.

The fairy tale I once dreamed about came to a crashing stop in June. My children were in Cookeville visiting their grandparents, so we went to hang out with a mutual friend. We pulled out of the driveway to head home when I got the phone call that sent me running.

Jane was on the phone, and she said we have a problem. I said, did we forget something and she says no; my daughter said Tony was fondling her when he put her to bed. I jumped out of the truck and started screaming. I called the police and started running. I didn't know where I was running, but I ran.

The next few weeks were a blur, but I managed to make Tony leave the house long enough for me to get my kids back home, so I could ask them the question I had been dreading for days. "DID TONY TOUCH YOU INAPPROPRIATELY?"

Flash Forward: This is my daughter's story to tell, so I am going to stop here and pick up a few days later.

I called my dad and stepmom. After listening to me, they put a plan in motion to come and get the kids and me. We left Panther Creek and moved into my stepmom's childhood home upon Coal Bank Road, in Sparta, Tennessee.

I had started going back to the Kingdom Hall, and I had made a few friends. Then all my old demons came after me. By day I was a mom, an upstanding citizen, but by night I was coming apart at the seams.

Kathy gave birth to her daughter in October. The kids and I were settling into the blue house on Coal Bank road. I was single for the first time in my life, and it felt good. However, my body did not want to, and I had several surgeries while trying to put my life back together. I also had two one-night stands with Ace and Kevin.

Ace gave me marijuana for the first time. I had no idea that Ace had laced it with pain medication. Ace was supposed to be my friend, but instead, he got me high and took advantage. I won't call it rape because I was an adult, and I knew better than to be alone with a man, but I seriously did not see this coming.

Edgar was in Ohio serving his prison sentence when he started writing to me. After a few months, he asked me to marry him. On Thanksgiving 2009, the kids and I made the trip to visit him. David and I were a hot mess and broken, but we still had life in us. We decided that it was the time that we stopped all the craziness and give our children the life they deserve.

I took this with my camera when we lived on coal bank road. Part of me was slowly dying.

CHAPTER THIRTY-THREE
Thirty-Third Year of my Life
"New Beginnings"

2010 and an earthquake hit Haiti killing more than 160,000 people. I have always been told that my life could have been worse. I think going back over the world events really makes me appreciate the life I've lived. No matter how bad it felt, it could have been worse.

It is a new year, and my life is again fixing to change, but I think it will be for the better this time. Edgar and I have been writing for months, and I have forgiven him for the adultery and the lies.

My stepmom read all his letters, and she gives me her opinion. I can always count on her to be honest with me. In March, she agreed to make the trip with me to pick up Edgar in Ohio. He was being released, and I was nervous.

It had been years since we were together, and we both had changed so much. I didn't sleep much the night before, so I went through the house trying to make sure everything was perfect. I had become quite a messy person over the last year, and Edgar had significant OCD.

When Edgar came home, we got remarried. I felt peace again. We reconnected, and I thought I could relax. We both were working, and the kids were thriving, or so I thought. We went to the kingdom hall every time the doors were open.

My grandma Abigail lived next door to my dad, so I got to spend many hours with her while the children were at school.

Edgar was home, so I didn't have to wait for phone calls or write letters to the prison. I saw hope again and prayed that this time everything would be okay. It was a culture shock to him, but he embraced it with an open heart.

We bought Jacob a new four-wheeler, and my mom came up from Georgia to visit. Jacob and I were working for my dad in the music store, and everything felt right.

I hated being in Sparta, but I didn't have to leave the mountain often unless it was to go to Crossville. I felt safe and secure, but my PTSD kept me in constant worry about the future.

I thought that maybe God had brought me back here to find peace and to heal from the past. I didn't question anything. I wasn't scared or worried about anything.

Thanksgiving came and went, and we were hopeful for the New Year. However, Satan had a different plan for my family. He was about to crush me to my very core.

Don't let history repeat itself.

CHAPTER THIRTY-FOUR
Thirty-Fourth Year of my Life
"Back to College"

2011 and a 9.0 magnitude earthquake hit Japan, triggering a tsunami that killed thousands of people and caused the second-worst nuclear accident in history.

This chapter is tough to write. My fingers are shaking. I wouldn't say I like bad memories, especially the ones that cut you to the core.

Satan was not finished hurting our family.

Flash-forward: An eighteen-year-old man raped my daughter. This tragedy is not my story to tell, so please understand that you will only get my viewpoint.

I started counseling, which helped me cope with everything. I felt like I had been raped all over again. It was my worst nightmare. I could feel it like it happened yesterday. My child had changed, and I knew the obstacles that we were going to face over the next few years. I was gazing at my mirror image, and she was full of rage.

I had made up my mind that no matter what my daughter did that, I would not force her to be married. I would walk with her through all the pain. It was easier said than done, and I made so many mistakes. I hurt for my daughter and myself. I could hear my parent's words flowing from my mouth, and I hated myself.

It was a horrible time in our family, but I did the only thing I could. I moved us back to Cookeville. I was accepted back into college, so the family moved to a duplex in Cookeville, Tennessee.

Edgar quit his job in Crossville to take a position in Cookeville, which paid more money. However, his work laid him off a few weeks later, and our lives were turned upside down. The TVA tried to repossess the truck and four-wheeler. Aaron's Rentals took our furniture.

I was glad to be in a better home and had even gotten another little dog. The stress from college and finances landed me back in the hospital. This year was terrible in my life, but I made it through. As the days passed, I cried more and more, but I decided to throw myself into college. It would be my release.

I had a few surgeries for the Hidradenitis Suppurativa, and I tried to pretend like everything was going to be ok. It wasn't long before Edgar, and I argued all the time about the kids. He always believed everything they said, but I knew they were getting involved with bad kids.

Once again, God was out of our lives, and Satan was running loose. My body started giving me more trouble, and my legs hurt all the time now.

I was in a play this year at the Back Door Playhouse at TTU. I love acting!

CHAPTER THIRTY-FIVE
Thirty-Fifth Year of my Life
"History Repeats"

2012 and tornados kill twenty-seven people in Indiana and Kentucky. I am trying to hold myself together, and I wasn't doing an excellent job of it. My sister had moved next door, and I was reaching out to old friends. I thought that it might help with my depression. I even started counseling.

When I say that my daughter was filled with rage, it is an understatement. I barely had the energy to keep up with her, and my body was falling apart more and more each day. I had no idea that I had Multiple Sclerosis, so I just shut down emotionally.

One evening on my way home from work, I called to check on Jasmine's ex-boyfriend. I heard that he was very depressed, and it was coming up on time to go visit the baby's grave. I picked him up and brought him to Cookeville to go to the movies with us as a family. I felt terrible for him as he seemed to be very depressed over the way his life had turned out. Then the unthinkable happened.

Morgan and I had a cold, and it had gotten worse that evening, so when we got home, we took cold medicine and went to sleep. Sometime in the early morning hours, Jasmine's ex-boyfriend raped Morgan! The next morning, I felt like I had a stroke, but there was no time to worry about myself. I had to process that my child had been assaulted not once, but twice, now.

Flash-forward: The above crime is not my story to tell. I can only share my experience during the events. This crime is a public record, and the man is now a registered sex offender.

You will see by my photo that I was struggling to smile. I became seriously ill and hospitalized. Then, I left college. I couldn't handle it all. My worst nightmare had come true, so while I was dying inside, I fought to keep my family from falling apart.

Dakota and Jacob were often forgotten because my mind focused on my baby girl. I tried to spread myself out to everyone, but I was thin as paper, so I did what I always do and turned to my drug of choice, and now, it was work. The family had opened a business, so I threw myself into it.

I worked for my father and stepmom running the family music store. Some days, it was more than I could take, so I shut down and became an automaton again. I know that my family loved me and were only trying to help, but I think I needed to see a therapist. I was coming undone, but I had also mastered the ability to "fake it until you make it."

The Hidradenitis Suppurativa started to clear up. I was wiping my body down with 95% alcohol every day. I did not know that it would hurt me, but it wasn't long before I started getting raw under my breast. I was so desperate to work because when I was working, I did not think about the sadness in my life.

One day, Kirk came into the music store with his wife. I tried to ignore it, but I couldn't help but think, "What if?" The year 1992 was so different from the life I live now. Then I remembered our last encounter in 1997 when I was living on Maple Avenue. That was enough for me to feel nauseous and walk into my office.

CHAPTER THIRTY-SIX
Thirty-Sixth Year of my Life
"Justice for my Child"

2013 and the more I look back in history and read my journals, the more I realize that bad things happen almost every day. It is time for some good news. Oh, I remember something. A two-year-old born with HIV was the first to be cured.

I was trying very hard to get us moved from the duplex. My sister was living next door, so leaving her was not going to be good for me. She was my best friend, and it was killing me to leave her to move somewhere else. Life was so confusing and stressful.

Dakota and Jacob helped me paint Morgan's bedroom, but it was an illusion. You cannot paint trauma away. We needed to move, but every house I found was either out of my price range, or nasty. Plus, most of the landlords checked your credit. Due to the bankruptcy, I couldn't see anything to make this nightmare stop.

I think I blocked out a big part of this year because I was working all the time. Morgan was running wild, and I didn't know what to do. Grown men were after my child. There were times I thought about killing someone, but I knew that my other children needed me. I continued to pray and stick to my plan. I would never sign for my child to get married.

Finally, the rapist was convicted and sent off to do a few years in prison. My rage intensified as I couldn't believe that he got only five years for rape, and my husband had received more time for worthless checks years ago. How can this crime not be a life sentence? We never get back what the criminal takes from us.

Then the worse night of my life happened. My baby girl attempted Suicide. I remember sitting all night on the hospital floor. I was in shock and begging God to take my life instead of hers. I know this sounds noble, but it was pretty selfish. I didn't want to live anymore, so I was more than happy to give up my life to save my child. I never stopped to think about anyone else when I had an episode. PTSD is evil, and my old demons loved to mess with me every chance they could.

I fell a few times this year and started having major speech issues. It seemed what I thought to say and what came out of my mouth were two different things. It scared me, but only because I knew my children needed me. I still thought about how dying would be the ultimate release.

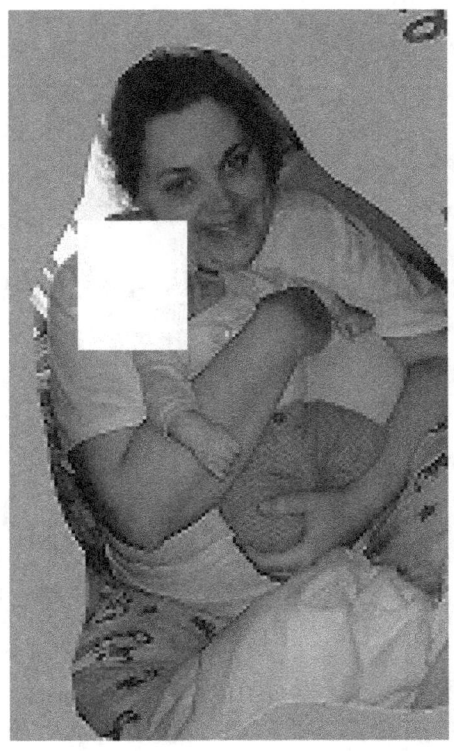

My youngest nephew was born!

Being an Auntie is Awesome!

CHAPTER THIRTY-SEVEN
Thirty-Seventh year of her life
"Sulfur Ridge"

2014 and we had the Ebola outbreak. The country was in a panic, and I was sad because Robin Williams committed suicide. Losing Robin made the world a darker place. His comedy could always make me laugh. I guess it only proves that he was a true actor.

Then came the Bill Cosby sex allegations. That was devastating because I loved his show as a child. I continued to ask myself questions like, "What did that say about me?" "Was I always going to be a target for men like that?" "Shouldn't I have seen it on his television show?"

This year would be the year that I have my all-time parenting fail. Edgar and I move to Sulfur Ridge Road. We meet John, and he was Dakota's fiancé's best friend. He was older than Morgan, but he had been through significant trauma; his father committed suicide. Morgan seemed so happy, and I was not about to ruin that with my conscience.

Dakota moved out because she could not handle the stress in the home. Troy's parents let her live with them, and she graduated high school. I felt a sense of peace. One of my children graduated from high school.

John gave us an option to move into his trailer, so we could leave the duplex. I jumped on this opportunity. We had several animals and needed to be out in the country.

Many people might judge me for this decision, but I wasn't signing for Morgan to get married. Morgan was a rape victim, so I pretty much let her do what she wanted as long as she was going to school and at home when I went to bed at night. I kept tracking apps on her phone, and we had parental controls through Verizon. She always thought we didn't know what she was up to, but I always knew she was in Cookeville. Her friends would message me when they got mad at her, so there wasn't much that I did not know.

My poor choices led to guilt. Morgan took her anger out on me, and so I felt even more guilt. The depression was terrible, but I focused on work to ease the pain.

We would spend Halloween in Flynn's Lick and Christmas in the mountains. Life seemed to be getting better, but Satan was just getting started. He had much nastier plans for us in the future.

Dakota Graduated High School!

2014

We always had the best time in the mountains. I wish now that I had never come back to Sparta. If only I knew then what I know now.

CHAPTER THIRTY-EIGHT
Thirty- Eighth year of her life
"I'm a grandma"

2015 and earthquakes, fires, hurricanes, and tornadoes are getting worse each year. There is so much more violence in the cities, so I am glad that we live in the country. Jacob spent much of his free time helping John clean up the property. There were old buildings and hundreds of tires that had to be cleaned up before his graduation party.

Jacob graduated high school and left for his trip out west. When he returned, he decided to forgo college and work for my parents. My dad decided to open another store, which would mean a move to Crossville. Everything went right in the beginning. Then Morgan went wild.

I had given up on trying to fight her when it came to boys. She dated who she wanted to, and as long as Morgan was at home at night, I felt she was safe. I felt like I was looking at myself in the mirror. No matter what she did, I knew that all this had to play out for her to heal.

We had been to so many different counselors, and from the internet to family, people attacked me for my choices, but I could only go on what I had experienced, so I continued to let Morgan be herself and act out her feelings. She had every right to be angry, and my love for her began to heal, even my wounds.

It wasn't long before summer turned to fall, and I felt a change coming. I prayed that it would be a good change, but I should have known better. Satan wasn't done with me yet. He had not broken me. I was still fighting to stay alive, and I always loved God.

This is one of the last photos I took with my grandma. I miss her so much.

Jacob made us all proud when he graduated high school. I wore the same dress every graduation.

Dakota got married and had a baby. I was officially a grandma. I know I have bonus grandchildren, but there is nothing like watching your own child bring life into the world.

2015 ended in a cloud of darkness as we lost Grandma Abigail. It still hurts so much. Morgan also had a miscarriage, and I had a small heart attack. No one knew what was wrong with me.

CHAPTER THIRTY-NINE
Thirty-Ninth Year of my Life
"Depression"

2016 and ISIS was killing more and more people. The word terrorist was on the news every day, and it was so depressing. Late one night, my mom called, and she needed our help. She was finally leaving my stepdad! She was moving back to Tennessee to live with my sister Kathy in Cookeville.

Morgan graduated high school, and we would meet our future son-in-law Edward. Edgar and I accepted my parent's offer and moved into their old house on Idlewild Drive, Sparta, Tennessee.

I was on cloud ten thousand. We were leaving the house in Crossville, and I could wake up to the beautiful view of the lake every morning. I started going to the doctor and finally getting all the tests done that I had put off from last year.

Nothing prepared me for what my CT scan suggested. The test results said possible Multiple Sclerosis. I had just started taking the Humira for the Hidradenitis Suppurativa, and my nodules were healing.

How could this be happening? I mean, it was also positive because now I knew what was wrong. It explained the numbness, speech problems, memory problems, and the pain I felt if I stood for an extended period. I tried to be optimistic, but the old demons of depression and anxiety were slowly creeping back into my mind.

Then, my dad's business started to suffer. I felt like it was all my fault, but I could not control what was happening. The banks had betrayed us on the loans, and we were at the mercy of the creditors. I stayed in constant stress over the finances. All of my old childhood demons came back, and I wanted to die.

Then, the MRI results came back, and I felt my life was over. Dr. Gaw sent me for a ton of blood work, and on my birthday, I underwent a lumbar puncture. He wanted to rule out everything else before he gave me the diagnosis of Multiple Sclerosis.

Morgan graduated a year early and moved into her own apartment. I was slowly becoming an empty nester. I was nervous, happy, scared, and depressed at the same time. I was delighted to be done with parenting, but was I really done? It's a trick. They multiply and come back, but you love them so much that you're happy to see them when they return.

   I stayed busy with yard sales. I had been given all of my grandmother's belongings except for furniture and coins. I was given her wedding bands, and I still wear them to this day. Kathy wears Grandpa Leo's wedding band. I sure wish they could see how beautiful their great-great-grandson is now. There is nothing better than sweet hugs and kisses from your grandchildren!

Getting Loves from Tigger always made me feel better.

Morgans graduation 2016!

Jacob and Lisa get married, and it was a fantastic event. I am so proud of them both. I wish it would have stayed this perfect.

Morgan was pregnant again and she looked so beautiful!

Edgar & I holding the baby bear in the Mountains!

CHAPTER FORTY
Fortieth Year of my Life
New York New York

2017 and Donald Trump is sworn in on January 20, 2017, as our 45th president of the United States. The news stations decide to start abusing drugs. HAHAHA, no, not really, but if you were sitting on this end of my television, you would think that they have all gone insane. I try to stay out of politics, but it is everywhere!

Dr. Gaw walked into the room. Edgar and my stepmom came with me to the appointment. He looked over the test, and he said this is the worst I have ever seen. There is no doubt you have Multiple Sclerosis. I do not remember being upset. The sadness on his face, Edgar's face and my stepmom's face was so shocking that I couldn't be upset. I was more worried that my family was going to fall apart.

I looked at the doctor, and I asked him what he would do if I were his daughter. He said, "Start treatment right away." Copaxone was a well-known drug, but it would mean more shots and more fatigue.

When we got home, my dad called me, and he told me that they wanted to take me on a cruise. The cruise would start my year of adventures. I went on a cruise with my parents in February, Morgan gave me a grandson in March, the family went on a camping trip in the summer, Morgan, and Edward would get married in August, and Jacob took me to New York in October.

I got to swim with dolphins, witness new life being born, see my daughter walk down the aisle, and walk the streets of New York City. It was during this time that I started using essential oils and changing my diet. I knew that Paleo would help the HS and possibly slow the progression of the MS.

Life happened so fast that I never had time to be depressed. I decided to write my book, and everything was falling into place.

November 24, 2017, brought about a cold evening, but it was warm enough to have the door open, and my thoughts have been on the business and my family.

Thanksgiving was over, so I was excited to watch my grandchildren play with the new toys that I had gotten on sale that week. Edgar just arrived home from work, and he was in the kitchen. I was sitting on our reclining couch listening to him talk about his day when he casually said to me, "Kirk came in the store today looking at an Ibanez guitar."

I didn't think much about it and shrugged it off, and then Edgar said: "Kirk's getting a divorce." I felt my chest stop. I couldn't believe it! NOT Kirk... A divorce? *No way*. He had been married for years.

I didn't say anything, but for the rest of the night, I Facebook stalked, Kirk. I finally broke down and sent him a message. It was a simple message telling him hello, and that I was sorry to hear that he was getting a divorce. My body filled with so many emotions. Faster than the speed of light, I was 14 again sitting in the backseat of my mother's car, and Kirk was staring into my eyes. Chills covered me, and I felt excited.

I looked around to make sure that Edgar didn't notice I felt a sense of guilt. I mean.... Who gets curious over the news that their high school boyfriend is getting a divorce? I kept telling myself that I am married and that it isn't normal for me to be feeling this way. I brushed off the teenage infatuation and decided that this could be my first interview for the book. I had blocked out so much of my life from 1992, so I thought that talking to Kirk would bring me some closure. If only I could have seen into the future and known that my heartache had just taken its first breath.

Later that evening, Kirk responded to my message. I honestly didn't think that he would because over the years I have tried to be friends with him, and he didn't want any part of it.

We talked most of the night, and it felt like we had never been apart. I was so confused yet happy. I felt like listening to music and singing the more I talked to him. I decided that I must see him face to face so that I could straighten out my feelings. I kept telling myself that I am married, and he is married! I have major health problems. Kirk still loves his wife.

When we discussed the end of our relationship, we both found out that my father had lied to me. I currently live next door to my father, so you can imagine this became a massive problem. I now blamed my father for every horrible thing that had ever happened to me.

If he had not scared Kirk and forced me to marry Troy, then I would not have endured years of pain. Learning the truth made me want to write the book more than ever before. I kept thinking that every ounce of love that I had spent years building towards my father had suddenly dissipated.

My dad always said the past is the past. He made one decision in my past that changed the very outcome of my life. Not for a few years, but for twenty-five years! I love my dad, but this was the final straw. I was sick of his lies and sick of him sweeping things under the rug like they hadn't happened.

I took hot baths and drove into my writing. I also wrote to President Trump and received a thoughtful reply from the President and First Lady. I keep it hanging on my wall as a reminder that the news media is not always factual when it comes to politics. All people lie.

I occasionally write the President with ideas coming from those of us who are disabled and the actual middle class. I also pray for him because I firmly feel that prayer can help those who are struggling.

Happy Memory from my first and last the cruise - 2017

My youngest child gives birth to a beautiful baby boy.

Dinner with my dad and sister - 2017

Autumn Acres with my nieces and nephews - 2017

My baby girl gets married August 4, 2017

Niagara Falls & Statue of Liberty

2017
October in New York City

West 35th Street

Visit to the Smoky Mountains

The choices you make can ruin your life, but they can also have a ripple effect for the next generations. Choose wisely! - Tina Milligan 2019

CHAPTER FORTY-ONE
Forty-First year of my life
"Truth is Pain"

2018 and the #MeToo movement is in full swing. Men are being arrested, and the media reports accusations almost daily. I just turned 40, and I am falling apart. Between the medication, Multiple Sclerosis, and finding out more and more truth about my past, I am a hot mess!

My heart is in a dangerous place, and I talk to Kirk every day. No, I did not cheat on my husband, but I came close. Lucky for me, my new drug of choice is writing. I no longer act out my anger in a sexual manner. Writing keeps my mind busy, and my legs shut!

It has been years since sex gave me a release. I don't know if that is a sign of healing, but I feel very positive about it. Kirk calls me Beth, and I can be around him without having uncontrollable sexual urges. I know that doesn't sound like much progress, but seriously, it is huge for me.

I don't drive much anymore, so I rely on social media to talk to friends and do interviews for the book. I recently found the little boy from Kindergarten, and our friendship has blossomed into something beautiful.

My sister is now my caregiver while Edgar is at work, and I use my laptop on days that I cannot get out of bed. I still have PTSD. When life gets hard, I have to stop and ground myself before I continue. I haven't made any more suicide attempts, but I do still think about dying when the pain is intense.

I write. I pray, and I eat. My life is very simple these days. It has been over a year since I went camping, and we do not go out of town anymore unless it is to see my doctors.

I pretty much stopped having anything to do with my dad. He closed the family business, and my son opened his own music store. I try to be respectful and put it behind me, but my mind is on new facts every day now.

Jasmine's son spent the summer with us. We went swimming, and I had the best time. I hope that it becomes a routine with us because he loves the water.

Jacob and Lisa blessed me with another grandson in August, and Dakota blessed us with our first granddaughter in November. I have grandbabies coming from all directions, and I love them so much. We had Thanksgiving with Jacob and his family this year, and we spent Christmas with Troy's family.

I made the decision to stop practicing all forms of religion. I have my relationship with God, and after I finish this book, I do not plan to discuss it with anyone, but God. I can feel him holding me as I take my first steps into freedom. I am learning that those who love you will not repeatedly hurt you.

Bray, I love you to the moon and back. Never forget Grandma Far, Far away. I loved our times at the pool and will always cherish the times I watched you jump into the deep waters!

Jacob & Lisa bless us with a grandson.

Dakota & Dan bless us with our first granddaughter.

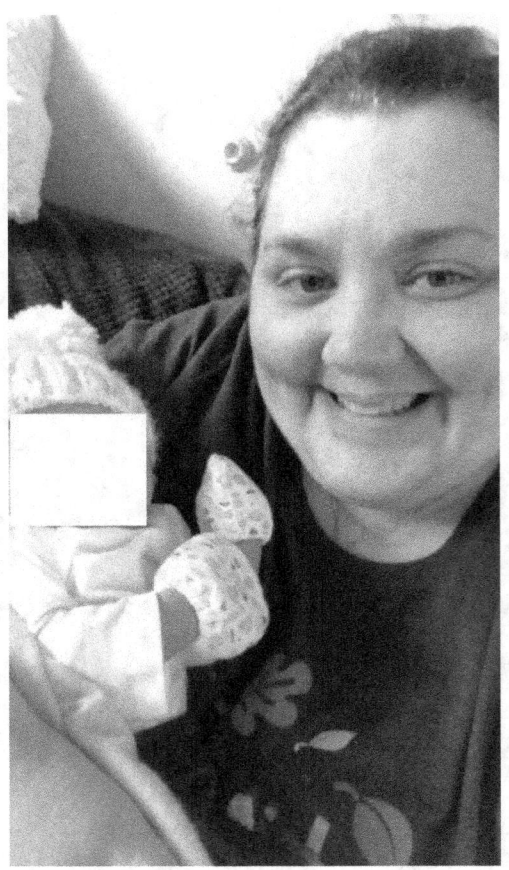

My life could have taken countless courses had I chosen differently at the numerous crossroads. I could be dead right now. I could have let the rage eat me alive to the point that I let go of everything I love. I could be in prison right now, but instead, I am here telling my story.

I do not have an exact remedy for you, except for one thing that has helped me. When you are confused, STOP, and ground yourself. Use discernment in all your choices. Rushing into anything can make your life worse. Pray, eat, and sleep before you make any radical changes in your life.

I am thankful to be here today. I have found through my writing that it wasn't the trauma that transformed me, but it was how I handled it that made me unstoppable. I didn't let it eat me! I found the strength to get up and try again.

I am human, and I am weak. There are times that I drink, curse, and get angry, but I am not fake. I will always tell you the good, bad, and the ugly so that you can see the full picture. That is what defines me as a woman.

In the end, I give all the credit to God. He never gave up on me, and he loved me through many dark times. If you do not believe in God, that is your right, but I know he is real. I see him in everything that I love.

THE END

2019 and President Trump is still in the White House. Tennessee has been struck with mass shootings. I am scared to go to the city or any place where there are tons of people.

The winter here has been mild, and my life has done a complete 180. Last week I spent a few days with my youngest daughter, then Edger, and I moved in with my son Jacob and his wife, Lisa. On April 2, 2019, I officially left the mountain. Things turned ugly when I let my stepmom read my book. I will save that story for my Blog.

Right now, I am editing this book and getting it ready for publication. I decided to set up all my online platforms and self-publish. I have started the "Best Bet Diet" and joined a Facebook support group. I now have a P.O. Box, so people can write to me or mail me things to try on my Vlog. My pets have taken over my Instagram, and TikTok is my addiction, because I use laughter to fight the pain.

I have Vlogs on YouTube, and I just rolled out the Podcast. I never know what I will wake up feeling as Multiple Sclerosis is so unpredictable. My main focus is on my family and grandchildren. I am 41 years old, and I have eight, yes, eight grandchildren. My sister is still my caregiver during the day, so on good days, we go on adventures and publish vlogs.

Jasmine blessed us with a new granddaughter. She is beautiful, and I can't wait to meet her! She was born with Down syndrome, but she is happy and healthy! I know Jasmine has a long road ahead of her, so I pray for her and her family every day. We haven't met my eldest stepson's children. Travel and relationship problems continue to be an issue, but that is not my story to tell.

I made the decision to leave Edgar and tell him the full truth about Kirk. Then I gave Kirk the last chance I will ever give him. I told him that I loved him, and he said that he did not have those type feelings for me. I, in turn, made the decision to put him in my past where he belongs.

In the end, Edgar is my biggest fan, and he loves me. He has been patient during this journey. We both understand that life is not always cut and dry. There are times that we have to work through difficult times to enjoy the good times. I am finally at peace with the past.

I have written a short story about my interviews and conversations with Kirk and Stephen. I am saving that for future publication in the Town Spring Flows Again, Anthology IX, written by the Cookeville Creative Writers Association.

If you're ever in Tennessee and would like to meet for coffee, drop me an email. I pray that you are having a fabulous day.

Inside the Writers Mind

    I hear my mom's words so clearly. "It's hard to trust, hard to be positive, and even harder not to overthink situations once you have been hurt." The struggle is so real for me, and I wonder if I will ever find the peace and security stolen from me so many years ago. Many things in this book have probably shocked those who I have known for years. I have told them parts of my story, but never had the fortitude to speak my truth in such a way that it cannot be unspoken. There is no delete button once it is in print.

    There are times that I want to slam the laptop shut and walk out the door. I feel like I am losing myself as though I am slowly disappearing. My memory fades more and more with each passing day, so I depend on my notes and interviews to put the puzzle pieces together. It doesn't help that my thoughts are so random that even I struggle to keep up with myself.

    To add insult to injury, I now have Multiple Sclerosis. I did not only tell you my story for my health because I think holding in years of pain can kill a person, but I pray it will help you to find peace in your own life. I hope you make better decisions and avoid my mistakes. I hope my words might even save a life.

*Pictures sometimes paint an illusion of reality.
They mask traumatic events, tragedy, and broken hearts.
So, the next time you look at a picture, remember that
things are not always what they seem".*

*Tina Louise Milligan
September 12th, 2018*

Health Summary

I was diagnosed with Hidradenitis Suppurativa in my twenties. Dr. Pitts found cancer when I was 24, which led to a full hysterectomy. During this time, I also had a nerve blocker for migraines. My symptoms were all over the place. One that sticks in my mind is Vitamin D deficiency. I was granted disability in 2004 after two years of endless paperwork.

I learned how to manage the disease, but every day was a new challenge. By 2016, I felt like I was going to die, but I had a new doctor, and he didn't give up until he found out why I couldn't feel my feet. Gary Burks ordered a head CT scan, and a new journey began.

The local hospital thought it was my heart, and I went through an unnecessary heart catheterization. Then, my doctor sent me to a neurologist, and he ordered MRI's, MRA, MRV, Doppler, Echo, test for HIV, Lyme disease, Lupus, and a Lumbar Puncture. The day came, and he looked so sad when he told me that I have Multiple Sclerosis. Honestly, I was relieved to finally have answers. I had spent years being a guinea pig for doctors, and now that it is over, I can focus on the root of the problem, which is diet.

www.ingramcontent.com/pod-product-compliance
Lightning Source LLC
Chambersburg PA
CBHW051355290426
44108CB00015B/2025